Written by Rob Robideau

ISBN-13 978-0-9850491-4-0

First Printing: May 2014

Printed in the United States of America

Table of Contents

Who is this book for?

When people think of security, privacy, and anonymity, many things come to mind. Some people think of cold war spies transmitting seemingly random strings of numbers from tiny transistor radios hidden in pens or watches while they hide in the shadows wearing a trench coat. Others think of drug dealers in wife-beaters with wads of cash and pockets full of burner phones trying to evade law enforcement and launder their ill-gotten gains while they cruise the streets terrorizing neighborhood children. More recently, many people think of whistle-blowers like Edward Snowden and those who have followed in his footsteps.

I have to admit that I did have several specific situations and use cases in mind as I wrote this book, but none of them involved criminal enterprise. Yes, as with almost any good tool, those outlined here in this book can be used for nefarious purposes. Fortunately, in many more cases, they can and will be used by law abiding citizens to protect assets, avoid social stigmas, and increase safety.

Incognito Toolkit is intended to compile and bring this critical information to people that may not have the time to do loads of research or even know where to look, yet need this information to deal with today's changing digital landscape.

The information in this book will be helpful for:

- Those who want to anonymously share critical information with law enforcement or the public without endangering themselves or their families

- Those who want to keep their communications and personal information safe from the ever growing population of scammers and hackers

- Witness protection program participants or victims of abuse who need a safe and untraceable way to reach out to friends and family

- Political dissidents, journalists, or missionaries who need to maintain anonymity while operating in oppressive countries

- Executives and business men whose communication security can make or break multi-million dollar deals

- Those who wish to publish about dealing with a medical issue, a very personal religious experience, or a memoir including stories of questionable activities as a youth

- Law enforcement officers or private investigators who want to know what methods people are using to maintain anonymity

- Celebrities, politicians, or anyone dealing with stalkers or constant attacks on their privacy

- Law enforcement officers who are undercover or operating in hostile environments who may be in need of secure and anonymous communications

Now it's up to you to figure out how to implement this information in a responsible and helpful manner.

Introduction

As an expat living outside of the United States for some time now, I was nonplussed when the aftermath of certain leaked NSA documents revealed that all email communication to and from the United States was almost certainly being monitored for certain keywords.

At first, I did nothing. After all, I have nothing to hide. My communications are mostly with family about the cute things the grandkids did on a given day, tracking information for recently shipped parcels, or innocuous, work-related communications, but something weird started happening.

I noticed that I had started unconsciously self-censoring my messages. Despite telling myself that my communications were innocuous and I had nothing to hide, I found myself examining my email to make sure. Certain words that I previously had no problem using in common conversation, started being switched to more bland words that might be less likely to trigger further scrutiny. I no longer felt comfortable using words like "surveillance", "NSA", or even "watching" or "tap". Call me paranoid, but the uncertainty caused me to change my behavior.

When I consciously noticed the changes that I had unwittingly made, I was disappointed in myself. I didn't think of myself as the kind of person who adapted and changed just to fit in and avoid making waves, yet that was what I was doing. The longer I thought about it, the more ridiculous I found it to be. I wasn't doing anything illegal. Why was I concerned about extra scrutiny?

As I led myself further and further down this line of reasoning, I recognized that, despite my best intentions and aboveboard activities, there were both unknown laws and secret laws that I could be unintentionally breaking. I'm no lawyer. I often don't have a firm grasp on the laws that I do know and pretend to understand, let alone every law that could possibly apply to what is discussed in my personal correspondence. What about international laws? Could this information be shared with the government of my country of residence? What if they are already monitoring my communications like the NSA?

Needless to say, this did not turn out to be a healthy line of reasoning and my paranoia only seemed to increase. Finally, I decided that the best course of action would be to communicate in a manner less likely to be monitored by the powers that be. This would allow me to stop my self-censoring and it might also free up NSA resources that otherwise might be wasted on me. Now they can spy more effectively on people like you!

My research following this decision led me to some eye-opening realities about the current state of privacy and anonymity on the public internet, or more aptly, their seeming lack of existence. In my copious research, I found a number of tools and methods that helped to provide me with a modicum of privacy that allowed me to start communicating without the self-censoring and paranoia that had become my norm. This book is my attempt to share what I have learned and help you find your way through a very complex collection of available information.

This book is not a political tirade against government surveillance or the state of privacy. This is a practical guide to using the internet for research, communication, shopping, and file storage without revealing your most closely guarded secrets to scammers, nosy neighbors and employers, intrusive internet service providers, email and other communication service providers, and governments.

I have attempted to approach the subject from a pragmatic point of view, rather than complaining about the current state of affairs: These are the realities of what is happening right now and here is what you can do to live your digital life in a more private manner.

If you are looking for resources for topics relating to privacy, anonymity, and encryption that delve further into the subjects than this book does, be sure to check out the recommended reading list in the appendix!

Anonymity on the Internet

What is anonymity?

an·o·nym·i·ty
/ˌanəˈnimitē/ ◄ʼ)

noun

> 1. the condition of being anonymous.
>   "most people who agreed to talk requested anonymity"

Ok, so let's define anonymous:

a·non·y·mous
/əˈnänəməs/ ◄ʼ)

adjective

> 1. (of a person) not identified by name; of unknown name.
>   "the anonymous author of *Beowulf*"
>   *synonyms:* unnamed, of unknown name, nameless, incognito, unidentified, unknown, unsourced, secret More

Anonymity is keeping your actions and activities separate from your true identity or an identity that is publicly known.

For a number of reasons, the entities that we encounter on the internet may want to connect your online persona, purchases, and activities to a known and "proven" identity. Sometimes it is to sell targeted ads. Other times, it is for law enforcement officials to connect a real identity to an online persona because of an alleged crime.

Most of us already have some sort of public persona. We are known to friends, family, insurance agents, banks, and governments by a certain name and set of identifiers. These identifiers may include a social security number, a driver's license photo, a reputation, a driving history, or a health history.

That's OK. Most people need a real and public identity that is connected to them. This identity is often required for driving a car, setting up bank accounts, getting health, life, or automobile insurance, traveling via air, getting internet service, getting a credit card, making money from publishing a book, or getting phone service. Sometimes you need your real identity to be connected to you so that it can lend credence or value to your words and actions in a particular venue. Your brother may not care about an anonymous email that that shows up in his email inbox, but if he knows that it is from his brother... You get the idea.

Often, it's not even out of necessity that we avoid anonymity. Sometimes we just want convenience. It can be a pain using services that help to maintain anonymity. Setting up, organizing, and using quite a few different email addresses for different services can be confusing and annoying. Using the TOR network can be slow. Heading out to off-site internet connections for various activities can be time consuming.

Anonymity is not convenient, but sometimes we want convenience. We want to be able to do a quick Google search from a mobile phone and we don't care about it being associated with our Google account that has our real name on it. Sometimes we want to be able to make an online purchase and have it shipped directly to our residence. Sometimes we want to share our accomplishments, activities, and cute pictures of kids on social networks. Because of this, we can't always be anonymous.

Don't feel bad about these activities or assume that because of them, you will never be able to do anything anonymously. This book will show you how you can enjoy the convenience of your well-established web service accounts and still act with anonymity in certain, specific cases.

While the clues and connections that you leave behind online are not always followed-up on, the breadcrumbs typically remain for government entities, hackers, or the like to string together if they really wanted to expend the time and effort to connect the dots.

You need to start from scratch when it comes to anonymity. One of the most important aspects of maintaining some form of anonymity is keeping your identity-connected accounts separate from the accounts associated with your anonymous identity. You can start anew right now and create anonymous identities.

Levels of Anonymity

There are varying levels of anonymity. Almost anyone can be found with creativity and the right resources. When you do more to safeguard your privacy, you are rewarded with a higher level of anonymity.

What level of anonymity do you require? That requires you looking into the future a little bit to anticipate the resources and tenacity of the person or persons that may be looking to connect you to your real identity in the future. Will it be an online retailer that wants to know your purchases so that they can offer you more targeted advertisements? Will it be a forum troll that you might offend? Will it be a business or corporation that can spend loads of money on a private investigator because you tarnished their reputation when you revealed some inconvenient fact? Will it be a government entity with the ability to obtain warrants, subpoena your ISP and online services, and access surveillance footage from your favorite free wifi coffee shop or library?

If you have some idea of who or what you are trying to protect your identity from and what resources they may have at their disposal, you will be able to enact the proper level of anonymity without going overboard and wasting your own time and resources.

Unfortunately, there is no way to tell exactly who you are trying to protect your identity from. Sometimes there are overlapping levels of anonymity. They aren't always so cut and dried. That forum troll you offended might happen to be an upper level NSA analyst with access to copious resources. You never know.

Be careful and do as much as you can to protect your anonymity!

Identity Verifications

Most services today require logins and many of them have very good reasons. They need to organize their information in some manner. They want to provide a personalized experience. They don't want other people to access your personal emails, purchase history, etc.

Unfortunately, there are many websites that require a login, yet provide no added value because of it. They require a login simply because they want your information and they want to track you as you use their service or browse their site. When they provide a free service, this is their prerogative. However, some creative people have come up with a workaround that works for quite a few sites. BugMeNot (*www.bugmenot.com*) is a service that compiles and shares login information for various sites so you don't have to register and provide your own information. They even have Chrome (*https://chrome. google.com/webstore/detail/bugmenot-lite/lackfehpdclhclidcbbf cemcpolgdgnb?hl=en*) and Firefox (*https://addons.mozilla.org/en-US/firefox/addon/bugmenot/*) extensions that can automatically fill in the shared login information for you.

Unfortunately, this model doesn't work for all types of web services and you will eventually have to create an account and deal with loads of questions about your personal information.

Identity verifications are one of the biggest obstacles to anonymity. Let's look at some of the challenges that they create and how we can deal with them. In order to achieve varying degrees of anonymity, it is in our best interest to make the breadcrumbs that we may leave behind as difficult as possible to string together and connect to our real identity. Let's look at the example of creating a new email account with Google.

When you get to the sign-up page, they request the obvious information like username and password, but they also want your name, gender, date of birth, mobile phone number, and a previous email address.

It is fairly easy to provide unverifiable and unlinked information for name, gender, and DOB(make sure the DOB puts the age above 21 years old), but the mobile phone number and previous email address almost always link back to you and they are often verified. In other words, you will need to provide a valid phone number and email address for them to send a verification SMS and email.

Name

First | Last

Choose your username

@gmail.com

Create a password

Confirm your password

Birthday

Month ⇕ | Day | Year

Gender

I am... ⇕

Mobile phone

▪ ▾ +49

Your current email address

Prove you're not a robot

☐ Skip this verification (phone verification may be required)

44845658

Type the two pieces of text:

C ◀) ❓

Location

Germany (Deutschland) ⇕

Phone Verification

Note: There are email providers like Yahoo and Hotmail that do not require a phone number, but this guide can also apply to and help you with other services that may require a phone number for verification.

Most people understand how difficult it is to get a phone that isn't able to be linked back to them. In the movies, they talk about "burner" phones that can't be traced and the bad guys just happened to pick them up at the local convenience store, but activating most prepaid phones requires some sort of identity verification and that verification means that it is actually connected to your true identity. Somewhere in the mobile service provider's records is information that can be linked back to you down the road.

This is not to say that there is no phone service available that doesn't require personally identifiable information. I'm actually quite confident that the opposite is the case, but how much time and money are you willing to spend to find them? If money is not a consideration, send your butler down to the nearest big-box store to pick up all the prepaid phones, work through the activation processes, and let you know which one didn't require a social security number, address, or credit card number. I would love to do the research and present it to you here, but because of constantly changing policies, procedures, and regulations in this industry, the list wouldn't remain up-to-date for long. I really can't make any specific recommendations.

Other problems like stored credit card transaction information and store security cameras are easily solved by using cash and a "disguise" like a baseball cap and sunglasses during the purchase.

Where I currently reside, a government photo ID and thumbprints are a part of the process of acquiring a prepaid mobile SIM card. A simple way to get around all this would be to find a young person off the street who is willing to buy and activate a SIM card for you for some cash.

If you do pick up a "burner" phone just for the account verification, don't use it for your other activities. You obviously don't want to make phone calls to phones that can be linked to your real identity in any way.

The simplest way to "game" all of this verification is to use a number that isn't actually yours at all. Have the verification text sent to a friend and call him for the information. In a crowded area with lots of waiting people like a coffee shop, hospital waiting room, or transportation hub (bus stop, airport, etc.) ask around until you find someone who will accept a text from "a friend" for you.

Technically, even in these situations, without proper precautions, the message could still be linked to you. People still have memories. Your friend's phone has a call history that might be matched to the SMS history. The list of possible connections goes on and on. These connections are extremely unlikely to be made, but they are remote possibilities.

Email Verification

Email addresses are a little easier to game when it comes to verification. Most people will use the most convenient or readily available secondary email address that they have had for some time from a major web services provider like Yahoo, Microsoft, or Google. Sometimes the chain may be longer than others, but most of these email addresses eventually lead back to an email address originally provided by an internet service provider who probably has your true identity and even address somewhere in their records.

There are a number of services that provide temporary or disposable email addresses for setting up accounts. These services work in a couple of different ways. Services like Mailinator (*http://www.mailinator.com/*) simply accept and keep any email directed at their domain: "xxxx@mailinator.com". You can go to their site and check the "address" without giving any information or logging in. You just type in the email address that you used.

To illustrate how to use this service, I will send an email to a randomly generated username: SdXhDP4mHWFHEPIA7aAo@mailinator.com.

Now we will go to the Mailinator home page and enter the randomly generated username that we used.

This will take us to a public "inbox" for this particular username. No password is required. If no email has been received by the particular address, it looks like this:

When the email arrives, it will look like this:

When you click on the email, you can read it:

This service requires no personally identifiable information. The downside is that anyone else can do the same thing and there is the remote possibility that someone else could end up viewing your email. To avoid people looking at the email you send to their domain, use a relatively long username randomly generated by Lastpass. Remember this service is for anonymity, not necessarily security. According to the site FAQs, "after several hours, all email is auto-deleted."

They don't forward emails. They don't bounce anything back or return any emails. Anything sent to an email address ending with @mailinator.com will be accepted. Mailinator (*www.mailinator.com*) would work quite nicely for any registration where you expect an immediate verification email that may require action on your part, yet don't mind the risk of someone randomly accessing your email. Mailinator uses numerous different domains in case you are blocked from using an email address with the Mailinator domain.

Here are several other services that operate much like Mailinator:

http://www.mytrashmail.com/

https://www.guerrillamail.com/

http://www.mailexpire.com/

http://www.tempinbox.com/

Spambox (*http://spambox.us/*) operates in a slightly different manner. They offer a temporary forwarding service that lasts a set amount of time:

They claim that they have "an automatic cleanup agent that wipes out every n-minutes the expired Spambox e-mails." For this service, you will have to provide your own email address, but it is never revealed to the service for which you are registering. They only see the temporary forwarding address that you give them. A similar service is offered by Jetable (*http://www.jetable.org/en/index*).

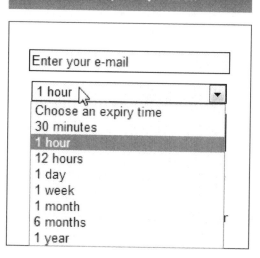

Behind the Scenes: IP Addresses

So we have talked about how to provide information that won't be linked back to your true identity, but these are just the information requests that you see. Behind the scenes, your browser provides all kinds of information when it requests a website. Much of it is necessary and understandable, but your IP address is one thing that is often collected that you should work to protect.

IP addresses are easily harvested, even by novices, using free and simple services like Clicky (*http://clicky.com/*):

There are numerous, seemingly innocuous ways to lure you to a website that can harvest your IP address. Check out "Pretexting Playbook" (*http://www.amazon.com/Instruction-Intentional-Misleading-Fabrication-ebook/dp/B00BHRMQ3O/persoarmam pod-20*) for an eye-opening revelation of creative methods to trick people into unknowingly giving away their identity. If you are accessing the internet from a place of business, the name of that business is often listed with the IP address. If you are accessing the internet from a personal residence, your ISP, city, state, and country are listed and available to anyone. From there, your address and personal information on file with the ISP can be subpoenaed by law enforcement or even revealed through coercion or simple social engineering techniques. Revealing your IP address can be very damaging.

Tor

You may have noticed that in the illustration of the Gmail sign-up page above, a German mobile phone prefix was suggested. This was based off of the IP address that they see. In reality, I am thousands of miles from Germany, but because I don't want them to record my real IP address, I use the browser pack from the Tor Project (*https://www.torproject.org/*):

The Tor Project is a network of nodes that route your internet communications through several different computers before they actually connect to the website that you are trying to access. Your signal could emerge from the network anywhere in the world.

TOR stands for "the onion router." TOR uses a protocol that is reminiscent of an onion because of the layered encryption and routing. Imagine a mailing an envelope. When it arrives at its destination, someone opens it and there is another envelope already addressed to a different person. This process happens several times until it eventually arrives at the final destination. Now, instead of envelopes, imagine securely locked boxes that can only be opened by each addressee. In this system, a single middleman/relay never sees or knows both the sender and the final recipient or the contents of the transmitted data. Technically, if a single entity introduced enough relays into the system, they could randomly end up being both your exit node and your entry point and connect you to the site that you are accessing, but this would be an extremely expensive and difficult proposition with no guarantee that you would actually be able to end up routing a specific person's traffic. Again, this is technically possible, but extremely unlikely.

For a more detailed explanation with illustrations, check out this page on the Tor website:
https://www.torproject.org/about/overview.html.en#thesolution

By default, the point where your transmissions emerge from the TOR network to head to their final destination, automatically changes every 10 minutes, making it appear to the websites you are visiting that you are accessing the site from an entirely new location. It is possible to configure TOR to only use exit nodes with IP addresses located in a specific country. To do this, you will need to edit the torrc config file located in the Tor Browser folder: **\Tor Browser\ Data\ Tor\torrc**

Open the torrc config file with your text editor of choice and add the line: "ExitNodes xxx" Replace the "xxx" with the exact IP address of the exit node you want to use or the country id in curly brackets. {bb} would indicate that I want to use an exit node located in Barbados. Here is a full list of the two-letter country codes:
https://en.wikipedia.org/wiki/ISO_3166-1_alpha-2.

Here is how it looks amended to the end of the torrc file:

```
SocksListenAddress 12
SocksPort 9150
ExitNodes {bb}
```

You also need to add one more line to the torrc file to keep Tor from automatically switching to a different country if all the exit nodes in the indicated country are unavailable or extremely slow. Add this line to the torrc file: "StrictExitNodes 1" The file should look like this:

```
Log notice stdout
SocksListenAddress 12
SocksPort 9150
ExitNodes {bb}
StrictExitNodes 1
```

With this line amended to the config file, if exit nodes are unavailable in the indicated country, Tor will simply stop working.

Recently, the infamous Silk Road was taken down by authorities. This was a buying and selling site hosted on servers that were only accessible through the TOR network. In other words, when you accessed the Silk Road site, at no time did your data travel through the open internet. Some privacy proponents were concerned that the TOR network had been compromised. While they are trying to take advantage of the fact that many people use Tor improperly, thanks to some recently leaked documents, it appears that the NSA has not been successful in compromising the TOR network. According to a leaked presentation (*http://epic.org/2013/10/nsa-attacked-tor-a-privacy-enh.html*) entitled "Tor Stinks", they will "never be able to de-anonymize all Tor users all the time."

It is important to remember that TOR alone won't keep you anonymous. You can circumvent the anonymity that TOR provides by using browser plugins, opening documents while online, and giving sensitive information to websites without an encrypted (HTTPS) connection. First, you should be careful to follow the very specific instructions from the good folks at TOR (*https://www.torproject.org/download/download.html.en#Warning*). They would, after all, know the best way to use TOR:

- **Use the Tor Browser** - Tor does not protect all of your computer's Internet traffic when you run it. Tor only protects your applications that are properly configured to send their Internet traffic through Tor. To avoid problems with Tor configuration, we strongly recommend you use the Tor Browser Bundle. It is pre-configured to protect your privacy and anonymity on the web as long as you're browsing with the Tor Browser itself. Almost any other web browser configuration is likely to be unsafe to use with Tor.

- **Don't enable or install browser plugins** - The Tor Browser will block browser plugins such as Flash, RealPlayer, QuickTime, and others: they can be manipulated into revealing your IP address. Similarly, we do not recommend installing additional add-ons or plugins into the Tor Browser, as these may bypass Tor or otherwise harm your anonymity and privacy. The lack of plugins means that YouTube videos are blocked by default, but YouTube does provide *the ability to use HTML5,* (enable it here: *https://www.youtube.com/html5*) *allowing you to watch some videos without using plugins.*

- **Use HTTPS versions of websites** - Tor will encrypt your traffic to and within the Tor network (*https://www.torproject.org/about/overview.html.en#thes olution*), but the encryption of your traffic to the final destination website depends upon on that website. To help ensure private encryption to websites, the Tor Browser Bundle includes HTTPS Everywhere (*https://www.eff.org/https-everywhere*) to force the use of HTTPS encryption with major websites that support it. However, you should still watch the browser URL bar to ensure that websites you provide sensitive information to display a blue or green URL bar button, include https:// in the URL, and display the proper expected name for the website. Also see EFF's interactive page explaining how Tor and HTTPS relate (*https://www.eff.org/pages/tor-and-https*).

- **Don't open documents downloaded through Tor while online** - The Tor Browser will warn you before automatically opening documents that are handled by external applications. DO NOT IGNORE THIS WARNING. You should be very careful when downloading documents via Tor (especially DOC and PDF files) as these documents can contain Internet resources that will be downloaded outside of Tor by the application that opens them. This will reveal your non-Tor IP address. If you must work with DOC and/or PDF files, we strongly recommend either using a disconnected computer, downloading the free VirtualBox (*www.virtualbox.org*) and using it with a virtual machine image with networking disabled, or using Tails (*https://tails.boum.org/*). Under no circumstances is it safe to use BitTorrent and Tor (*https://blog.torproject.org/blog/bittorrent-over-tor-isnt-good-idea*) together, however.

- **Use bridges and/or find company** - Tor tries to prevent attackers from learning what destination websites you connect to. However, by default, it does not prevent somebody watching your Internet traffic from learning that you're using Tor. If this matters to you, you can reduce this risk by configuring Tor to use a Tor bridge relay (*https://www.torproject.org/docs/bridges.html.en*) rather than connecting directly to the public Tor network. Ultimately the best protection is a social approach: the more Tor users there are near you and the more diverse their interests, the less dangerous it will be that you are one of them. Convince other people to use Tor, too!

The most secure way to use Tor is with the Tor Browser that comes pre-configured in the Tor Browser Pack (*https://www.torproject.org/download/download-easy.html.en*). You can use extensions to configure your primary browser to use Tor, but if you are like me and often want to use your browser in a non-anonymous manner, it can be a pain checking all your settings and disabling all plugins each time you want to be truly anonymous. It is much easier to simply open a new and pre-configured browser that was designed for anonymity.

Dealing with Tor Limitations

Because many email providers require you to use Javascript when you sign up for an account and Javascript makes Tor vulnerable and can possibly give up your true IP address, it might be wise to access the internet from a public hotspot when you open the account. Be sure that you are using an HTTPS connection so that your connection is encrypted and hidden from other hotspot users.

From that point forward, you can access the email using POP or IMAP via an email client configured to use Tor. If you are using Mozilla Thunderbird, there is an extension called TorBirdy (*https://addons.mozilla.org/en-us/thunderbird/addon/torbirdy/*) that makes the Tor configuration quite simple. Here is more documentation on TorBirdy (*https://trac.torproject.org/projects/tor/wiki/torbirdy*).

> "TorBirdy enforces the preferences it sets and attempts to change them using Thunderbird's settings or the configuration editor will not work as all such changes will be discarded when Thunderbird restarts. This is because we believe that these preferences should not be changed, whether deliberately, by mistake, or due to another extension, as doing so can compromise your anonymity. There are, however, some preferences that can be changed, and they can be accessed through TorBirdy's preferences dialog. Please note that if you are not an advanced user, you should NOT change any setting unless you are very sure of what you are doing."

If you open an email account from a physical location that cannot be linked back to you and you are careful to only access the email itself via Tor, that email provider should not have any IP address on file that can be linked back to you.

On a slightly different, yet related note, you need to remember that while this protects your IP address, it in no way conceals the actual content of your emails. If you want the email account to remain truly anonymous, you need to make sure that any emails with personally identifiable information are encrypted before they are received by your email provider's servers. Because most online shopping systems do not support sending encrypted email, you shouldn't use an anonymous email address for online shopping where you would receive unencrypted receipts with your personal information. I recommend using the combination of GnuPG and Enigmail with Thunderbird in combination with Tor/TorBirdy.

Tor is a fantastic and ingenuitive tool for anonymity, but it must be used properly and if you are lax in your usage, you can easily reveal your IP address and identity.

To check whether or not Tor is working or to check what is being displayed as your current IP address, you can use the following two pages:

https://check.torproject.org

http://whatismyipaddress.com/

Tor Hardware

One of the biggest drawbacks to using TOR is the difficulty of setting it up and making sure that everything is configured properly so that you aren't leaking information. Many people lack confidence in their ability to properly set-up and configure TOR, so they don't bother. Several entrepreneurs have recognized this as a business opportunity and are coming out with pre-configured devices for using TOR.

Safeplug (*https://pogoplug.com/safeplug*) is a $50 hardware device that you can connect to your router and allow you to browse "anonymously" via the TOR network. They claim that the setup only takes 60 seconds. This sounds like a great idea to help TOR become more mainstream and put to bed the commonly held myth that TOR is only used by criminals, but there are certain aspects of aspects of web browsing that could not be protected by a device alone. At this point, the device hasn't been fully vetted and I can't fully recommend it.

In order to use a hardware device like this effectively, users should also understand the impact and importance of using SSL as well as various browser cookie settings. Otherwise they could be quickly and easily de-anonymized by a dedicated third party.

This hardware could be good for someone that has the tech know-how to plug the remaining holes, but if you already know that much, why don't you just set up and configure it on your own computer?

Virtual Private Networks (VPN)

A VPN is particularly helpful when you are connecting to the internet from a network or internet connection that you don't really trust. A VPN service creates an encrypted tunnel direct from your computer to the VPN server in a different location. From the point that your communications leave the VPN service and enter the open internet, they are no longer protected or encrypted.

A VPN provides you with a certain level of privacy over the initial portion of the distance that your internet communications will cover. While using a VPN, your IP address will appear to be that of the server where your communications exit the VPN encrypted tunnel into the open internet.

If you are in an environment like an open wifi access point where you suspect people might be snooping and trying to intercept your communications, a VPN connection is a wonderful way to encrypt your communications until they are out of the "dangerous" area.

In the wake of laws requiring ISPs to record and keep logs of the most recent 18 months' *worth of subscriber activity (http://www.pcworld.idg.com.au/article/388021/new_u_bill_requi res_isps_keep_18-months_records/)*, people are looking for ways to keep their internet activity private from their ISPs that can easily be coerced into providing personal data to law enforcement officials for frivolous reasons.

While a VPN does mask your original IP address, most of the time, it won't make you truly anonymous because most good VPNs are paid services, and they will more than likely have your personal information on file if a government agency or someone with sway came looking for it. In this case, leaving the VPN's IP address unmasked is not a good idea if you want to remain anonymous.

Be sure to check out the section on anonymous financial transactions to find out how you can purchase VPN service without revealing your personal information.

There are a number of reputable VPN services out there, but here are a few that I have personally used or heard good feedback about:

GigaNews
http://www.giganews.com/

ProXPN
http://proxpn.com/

Ipredator
https://www.ipredator.se/

StrongVPN
http://strongvpn.com/

Rob Robideau

WiTopia
https://www.witopia.net/

Protection from Honeypot Hotspots

Less-than-scrupulous people have been known to setup unsecured wireless connections specifically in an attempt to obtain usernames and passwords that people may unwittingly transmit in an unencrypted manner.

Firesheep (*http://codebutler.com/firesheep/*) received a lot of publicity (see *http://lifehacker.com/5672313/sniff-out-user-credentials-at-wi+fi-hotspots-with-firesheep*) over the fact that it allows pretty much anyone to install a simple Firefox extension and harvest usernames and passwords for common web services like Google, Facebook, Twitter, Dropbox, Amazon, Evernote, and more from people that are using the same unsecured wifi hotspot and not encrypting all their communications.

An inexpensive LAN tap device (*http://hakshop.myshopify.com/ products/throwing-star-lan-tap-pro*) can be used in conjunction with a free program like Wireshark (*http://www.wireshark.org/*) to monitor network traffic and find out all sorts of information.

VPN services can protect you from these threats by creating an encrypted tunnel to transport your communications to a different location before sending them out over the open internet. Browser extensions like KB SSL Enforcer (*https://chrome.google.com/webstore/detail/kb-ssl-enforcer/ flcpelgcagfhfoegekianiofphddckof?hl=en*) and the EFF's HTTPS Everywhere (*https://www.eff.org/https-everywhere*) can also help by forcing your browser to use SSL and HTPPS to encrypt your communications whenever possible.

TOR and VPN

You could use the Tor Project from the point that you emerge from the VPN to protect your anonymity if you are using a VPN that has your real personal information on file. Using a combination of a VPN and TOR is not redundant. The VPN will encrypt and protect your communications from those attempting to intercept your communication at the source and TOR will make it difficult for those attempting to spy by backtracking from the site you are communicating with.

DIY VPN

If you have a connected computer in a separate, safer area, you can use it to roll your own VPN with services like Neorouter and Hamachi.

http://www.neorouter.com/

https://secure.logmein.com/products/hamachi/

Bear in mind that if your name is on the bill for that internet connection at the end of the DIY VPN, it doesn't really help you with anonymity, just privacy from those who may be trying to snoop on you from point you are first connecting to the internet.

Browser Fingerprinting

Text, data, and IP addresses aren't the only things used to identify you. If you have a unique browser configuration, a website can tell that your anonymous identity is using the exact same browser as your real identity used an hour ago to log in at this particular site.

Head on over to *https://panopticlick.eff.org/* and see how unique your browser's fingerprint is.

Within our dataset of several million visitors, only **one in 1,748,333 browsers have the same fingerprint as yours.**

This was the result of running the test in the TOR browser. Yes, it is keeping my IP address from leaking and refusing cookies, etc., but because the settings are so unique when compared to other users, my browser is extremely unique.

That being said, I tested an almost-stock Firefox browser and because of all the information that it was leaking, the fingerprint was twice as unique!

This site will show you what specific information is being revealed by your browser from your screen resolution and color depth to installed fonts and your browser settings.

If I used this same browser to log in with two different accounts for my real identity and my anonymous identity, the unique browser fingerprint could link the two of them.

A simple workaround could be to use a different browser when you are attempting to use the internet anonymously than when you are working with accounts that are linked to your real identity, but you can only install so many browsers and you will often need to use several different anonymous logins on an individual site. In these cases, even changing the size of your browser window will change your fingerprint slightly.

Here is a PDF put out by the EFF with tactics to defend against fingerprinting (*https://panopticlick.eff.org/browser-uniqueness. pdf*). Beware! There is lots of math-speak, but they do end up recommending TorButton (*https://www.torproject.org/torbutton/*) and NoScript (*https://addons.mozilla.org/en-US/firefox/addon/ noscript/*) for reducing fingerprinting.

Cookies

A browser cookie (*http://en.wikipedia.org/wiki/HTTP_cookie*) is a piece of data sent out by a website and stored by your browser that allows the website to remember things like what you put in your shopping cart or whether or not you are logged in. Tracking and third-party tracking cookies often collect data over time about the websites you visit. In a perfect world, we wouldn't accept any cookies, but there are many websites that require you to use cookies.

If you use something like the incognito mode found in the Chrome browser, all cookies and history from your session are automatically wiped when you close the window.

Personally, I use a free piece of software called CCleaner (*http://www.piriform.com/ccleaner*). It gives you some granular control over what data it clears from specific browsers and other apps:

My favorite feature is that you can get even more specific in which cookies are kept or cleared. You can select certain cookies and tell the program that they should never be deleted.

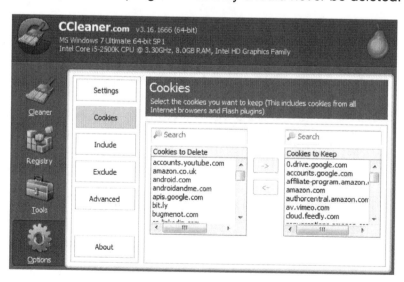

I also setup the program to run at startup and automatically close after the cleaning is done. This way, every time I start the computer, all extraneous cookies are cleared, but I don't have to re-log-into all of my most-used sites.

Cookies

    ○ Allow local data to be set (recommended)

    ○ Keep local data only until I quit my browser

    ◉ Block sites from setting any data

    ☑ Block third-party cookies and site data

    [Manage exceptions...] [All cookies and site data...]

Most browsers have settings that allow you to keep your browser from accepting any cookies, but, again, many sites require cookies. You should, however, have no problems with blocking all third-party cookies and site data. If you clear all your regular cookies on a regular basis, it still keeps the sites from collating any real amount of data.

Off-Site Internet Connections

You will see this term mentioned several times throughout the book when talking about ways to keep your real, home internet connection IP address a secret. Obviously, the best way to keep your home internet connection's IP address a secret is to not use it. This is the digital equivalent of using a phone booth instead of a personal phone. Before you head off to use just any internet connection though, I want to specify exactly what I am talking about when I use this term and what you should be looking for.

First, you want a connection that doesn't require some sort of registration. Don't use a library connection that might require your library card number. If you have to pay for the connection with a credit card or even log in using a code off of a receipt that might have your payment information, there is still a connection to your real identity. If you are purchasing something while using the hotspot, use cash.

Try to avoid using the internet connection at establishments that have surveillance cameras. A savvy investigator that traces your activity back to that particular establishment could find a way to access the recordings and scan the footage around the time of the activity.

Don't limit yourself to just coffee shops and libraries. Pick up a wifi hotspot sniffer or finder to keep an eye out for wifi hotspots anywhere. This Canary Wireless model (*http://www.amazon. com/gp/product/B0016LG6WS/ref=as_li_ss_tl?ie=UTF8&camp= 1789&creative=390957&creativeASIN=B0016LG6WS&linkCode= as2&tag=persoarmampod-20*) will not only show you the strength of the signal, but also whether the hotspot is "open" or "closed".

It's a pretty small unit, so you could carry it with you as you walk your dog through a neighborhood to check out potential wifi access sites. Later, you could come back in a car for a few minutes to use the connection.

If you have a smartphone, you can pick up an app that can perform the same function, but with a few additional features. Aptly named Wifi Finder (*http://v4.jiwire.com/search-hotspot-locations.htm*) for the both Android (*https://play.google.com/store/apps/details?id=com.jiwire.android.finder*) and IOS (*https://itunes.apple.com/en/app/wi-fi-finder/id300708497?mt=8*) platforms not only allows you to scan for hotspots, but also gives you access to their database of over 830,000 mapped hotspots in 145 different countries.

Not only is it illegal to access networks without authorization (*http://en.wikipedia.org/wiki/Legality_of_piggybacking*), but it probably would NOT be a good idea to just use your next-door neighbor's wifi. You want to make sure that you don't use internet connections that you might be peripherally connected to. The obvious place for investigators to look would be the neighbor, you. For obvious reasons, don't use the internet connection at your office or a family member's home.

You also want to avoid using several different hotspots that would essentially triangulate or create a pattern around your residence. Try not to settle into any repeating pattern that could give you away. For instance, don't settle into using the same coffee shop hotspot every Thursday during your lunch break. Someone could simply stake out the site and wait for you at the appropriate time.

If you don't choose an off-site connection spot wisely, you may end up leaving behind some easy clues and you might as well be using your own home internet connection. Be careful!

Monitoring your Public Persona

Most people have some sort of public persona that exists online. It is in your best interest to monitor online activity surrounding this publicly known persona. If there is some sort of connection made between the online activity that you are trying to hide and your public persona, you want to know so that you can head it off at the pass. If your personal information is revealed on the web, you want to know so that you can take actions that will limit your trouble and inconvenience down the road.

It could be something simple like a family member who happened to mention you and your hometown in a public Facebook post, or it could be something more malicious like someone publicly posting your telephone number and asking the masses to harass you. In the first situation, you could quickly message the family member and ask them to edit or remove the post. In the second situation, you could try to have your number taken down or get your number changed quickly.

Unless you have taken steps to monitor your public image online, you might never know about these security breaches until it is too late. Enter Google Alerts (*http://www.google.com/alerts*). Google Alerts allows you to set up a persistent search with notifications via email or RSS. You can set up alerts for you, your family members, your business name, or whatever. If there are new search results for your query, you will be notified.

Alerts

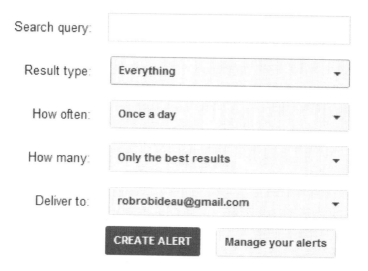

Many people call this a "vanity" search, but improper monitoring and management of your online persona can have some very serious security related consequences.

Locking Down Your Devices

Before you start worrying about the security of your data on the internet, you should start by making sure that your data is secure on your own computer and devices. Lock them down!

Accessing your phone should require a password. Logging into your computer should require a password. Your screensaver should require a password. Accessing your hard drives and USB sticks should require passwords. Are you starting to get the idea?

You should password protect your operating system user account, but I really recommend encrypting and password protecting each hard drive with Truecrypt (*http://www.truecrypt.org/*), especially the system drive.

If your computer or external drives are relatively portable, you may want to lock them down with a steel cable attached to something solid like a heavy desk. This won't stop a dedicated thief, but it will make a quick snatch and grab next to impossible. Kensington (*http://www.kensington.com/kensington/ us/us/s/1374/security.aspx*) has an entire line of locks dedicated to computers and their peripherals.

You should also keep an eye on your devices to make sure that they are not tampered with. Hardware keyloggers (USB or PS2) (*http://www.amazon.com/mn/search/?_encoding=UTF8&camp= 1789&creative=390957&field-keywords=keylogger&linkCode= ur2&tag=persoarmampod-20&url=search-alias%3Daps*) are fairly inexpensive, easy to connect, and unobtrusive enough to miss if you aren't looking closely. Make sure that there are no extra dongles, adapters, or cords that you didn't put there.

A dab of fingernail polish or paint on the edge of the heads of the screws on your computer case could alert you if someone opened it and tampered with the components. A very small piece of paper placed carefully just inside the case of a mobile device so that it would fall out when opened could be an indicator for smaller devices.

Mobile devices are easily cloned and switched out. A small, but inconspicuous mark on your mobile device will allow you to easily verify that the device you are using is really yours and not a clone with spyware.

If you are really paranoid, you could install a hidden keylogger on your own machine to monitor its possible usage by third parties. You can check for activity during times that you know that you were not using your computer. You are essentially using spyware on "yourself." There are several different keyloggers that should remain hidden and do the job (*http://www.raymond.cc/blog/free-and-simple-keylogger-to-monitor-keystrokes-in-windows/*).

Be aware that antivirus programs will view a keylogger as malicious software and you may have to click through a number of warnings before you are allowed to install the software. This would indeed be unwanted software if it were being installed by anyone other than you.

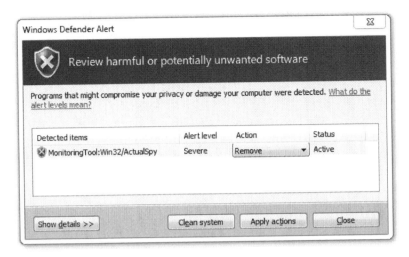

Along the same lines as a keylogger, you might want to monitor and limit the digital communications of your device. You might be surprised at how many programs "phone-home" from your computer for various reasons. Most often it is because of copy-protection measures, but many programs send out "anonymous" usage data to the developers so that they can find out how to make the software better. While this sounds innocuous enough, most often, you don't know exactly what information is being sent and how it might be linked to you via serial numbers or other means.

I use a small, lightweight program called TinyWall. TinyWall (*http://tinywall.pados.hu/features.php*) is a firewall application that by default blocks every program and keeps them from accessing the internet. You can approve individual processes or executables and allow them internet access. This will help to make sure you aren't unwittingly leaking information.

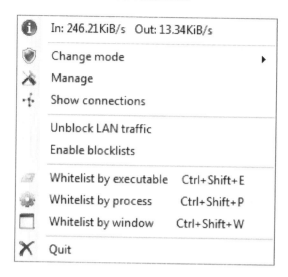

If you suspect that someone might be physically accessing your computer while you are away, you can set up a hidden camera to keep an eye on the computer while you are gone. Newer cameras like the Dropcam Pro (*http://www.amazon.com/gp/product/B00F9FCW7K/ref=as_li_ss_tl?ie=UTF8&camp=1789&creative=390957&creativeASIN=B00F9FCW7K&linkCode=as2&tag=persoarmampod-20*) can be setup to automatically alert you and highlight the recorded segments when people are moving or active in a certain area. You can set the camera to highlight the recording and let you know if people are in the vicinity of your computer. This will keep you from having to review all the footage manually.

The Dropcam Pro is not a hidden camera, but with a little creativity, you could stuff it inside a teddy bear or hide it in a book, etc.

The physical security of the devices that you use to work, communicate, publish, research, and store data, is paramount. If someone is able to take possession of or compromise your physical devices, the rest of the procedures and steps I outline in this book won't do you much good.

Passwords

Passwords are like keys for all the digital services you use. Just as simple keys are simple to replicate, simple passwords are easy to guess or brute-force. Your passwords should be strong, random, different for each account, regularly rotated, and well organized.

Creating Strong Passwords

Bear in mind that not every service will allow you to use 100 character long passwords with letters, numbers, and symbols, but your goal should be to make every password as random, long, and complicated as possible.

One way to consistently create random passwords that meet the requirements of whatever service you happen to be using is the Lastpass password generator:

You can set the desired length of the password and choose what kinds of characters should be included. I use this tool often as I create accounts with different services. It would be quite a pain to attempt to generate random passwords on my own by randomly mashing the keyboard and pressing the shift buttons or attempting to create a random string of numbers, letters, and symbols on my own. Because of this difficulty, many people default back to a common password or some variation of it with an amended section. While this is technically better than using the same password across multiple accounts, it will be pretty easy for any "guessing" computer program to figure out a simple variation. The password generator allows you to consistently and easily create complicated, random passwords with the click of a button.

Generating Random Personal Information

Sometimes you will need to provide more than just a username and password. Some services require other personal information like addresses, phone numbers, social security numbers, birth dates, and the list goes on. Only you can decide whether the information is genuinely required for a given service to properly function. Often, these services want this information merely to verify your identity in the case of a lost password. In such cases, it would be in your best interest to provide fictional data. There is no reason to put your personal information on another random server just so that they can have a security question that sets their mind at ease. In most cases, you can always update the information later if you find that they actually do need your personally identifiable information for a good reason.

For such situations, I recommend a service called a Fake Name Generator *(http://www.fakenamegenerator.com/gen-male-us-us.php)*:

You can set up the generator to create completely random international names and personas or focus on a specific gender, nationality, etc. It will provide you with a plethora of random information to associate with the identity including a made up email address, credit card information, physical address, phone number, vehicle, blood type, height, weight, and more.

It will look something like this:

Charles L. Jung
1829 Elk City Road
Indianapolis, IN 46204

Curious what **Charles** means? Click here to find out!

Logged in users can view full social security numbers and can save their fake names to use later.

 Sign in

Phone:	317-988-3854
Email Address:	CharlesLJung@jourrapide.com
	This is a real email address. Click here to activate it!
Username:	Whow1979
Password:	ou5Ahth1ae
Mother's Maiden name:	Espinosa
Birthday:	January 16, 1979 (34 years old)
Visa:	4716 8316 7201 3021
Expires:	3/2017
CVV2	380
SSN:	303-40-XXXX
	You should click here to find out if your SSN is online.
Occupation:	Molder
Company:	Little Folk Shops
Website:	Firmchair.com
Vehicle:	2000 Chevrolet Tahoe
UPS Tracking Number:	1Z 777 379 65 8762 501 3
Blood type:	O+
Weight:	153.8 pounds (69.9 kilograms)
Height:	5' 10" (177 centimeters)
GUID:	8ff81780-9c8c-49a3-bb62-1e5187b3feea
Geo coordinates:	39.808357, -86.157778
QR Code:	Click to view the QR code for this identity

If you login via a Google account, you can view full social security numbers and save profiles for later.

Because you will need to store this information somewhere, this option is quite convenient, but you should bear in mind that in the future, technically, these identities could be tied to whatever Google account you use to login in here. You might want to create a random Google account that cannot be linked back to you for use with this service.

If you don't want to go to the trouble of creating a new and unconnected Google account for use with this service there are other ways to keep track of a fictional identity. You could do something as simple as copying it all into a spreadsheet or text file, but I recommend using Lastpass.

There is a function of Lastpass that allows you to create multiple "Form Fill Profiles". This allows you to input and store all sorts of data about a fictional profile and keep track of it all in one place. You can name each profile in a way that will help you remember what it was created for. As an added bonus, you can easily have Lastpass use this profile to automatically fill in forms down the road. You also have all the information in one place without creating a new account to worry about with a new service. The downside to using your Lastpass account for this is that you will have to type the data into individual data fields. There is no copy and paste or one-click button to save it for later.

In reality, if you plan to use the data, at some point you will need to type or copy-and-paste the individual pieces of information into the appropriate data fields. You can do it now with Lastpass and let it auto-fill later or you can save it quickly and easily now with a single click and do all the data entry later when you actually use the profile. It's up to you.

Whenever you use a fictional profile for a particular account, you should note on that profile what it was used for and remember what can be linked to that set of fictional data. Every Lastpass form fill profile has a section for notes:

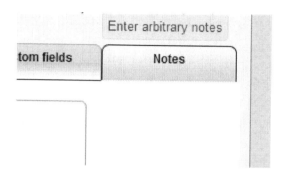

Rotation

I recommend regularly changing the password on your most important accounts. Over time, your password may have been inadvertently passed to a third-party who used a given account for verification. It may have been inadvertently saved by a browser if you used someone else's computer. You may have jotted it down and left it lying somewhere. The list goes on. There are numerous ways for bad guys to access passwords from keyloggers to temporarily accessing your mobile phone. Regularly changing a password gives you a fresh start and blocks anyone who might have had access to your password in the past.

You may not think that this is absolutely necessary, but most of the time when a password is revealed, it is without the knowledge of the user. It is in the best interest of the hacker/bad guy to keep the password theft a secret so that information and accounts can be accessed before passwords are reset. Regularly reset your passwords, even if you think they are secure. Schedule, weekly, bi-weekly, monthly, or quarterly password rotations and set them up as repeating events on whatever calendar service you use.

Google Calendar makes it easy to set up a repeating event to remind you to rotate passwords:

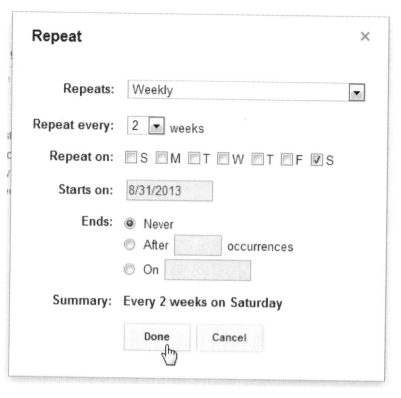

You can set the event to repeat at whatever interval you so choose based on a chosen number of days, weeks, months, or even years and send you a reminder email as the event approaches:

Reminders   Email ▾   10 minutes ▾ ×

Different passwords for each account

While I recommend that your key encryption system function in such a way that it never actually transmits your password over the internet or stores it anywhere other than your own locked down computer, there are obviously many different kinds of services that require an internet login of some sort. Even the best of these services are occasionally hacked and personal data is revealed.

If you read this article (*http://arstechnica.com/security/2013/05/ how-crackers-make-minced-meat-out-of-your-passwords/*), you will get a better idea of how easy it can be for hackers to guess and figure out your passwords that are stored on the servers of your web services providers. In this article, of the more than 16,000 "cryptographically hashed passcodes", 90% were cracked by a computer that spent 20 hours running a program specifically designed to figure out passwords.

In short, you shouldn't typically expect your passwords that are stored online to remain a secret forever. If you use the same password for all your accounts, it will be easy for a malfeasant to use those credentials to log into multiple online services and harvest information. If you used completely different, random passwords for each service, this is not an issue.

Organization

The more complicated and random our passwords become, the more difficult they become to remember. Thankfully, there are secure methods of keeping them all organized and easily accessible. The service that I recommend for this is Lastpass. Lastpass is a free service, but they have premium services and functions that are available for $12 per year. Most users will not require premium services and functions.

In short, Lastpass offers browser extensions, a web interface, and mobile phone apps that will help you create, keep track of, and synchronize your usernames, passwords, and other sensitive information across all your platforms. If you create an account on a website on your laptop and save it to your Lastpass "vault", when you attempt to access that website later on your desktop computer, the browser extensions will have synced and should already have the information ready for you. You can even set the extension to automatically fill in the username and password on certain sites.

What about the security of such a system? How can it be secure for our passwords and most personal data to be synchronized from platform to platform via the web? Please allow me to quote Lastpass on this:

1. All encryption and decryption happens on your computer.

When you create your LastPass account, an encryption key is created on your computer (your Master Password, or MP, and email go through a complex, irreversible process known as hashing to form your encryption key). Any sensitive data you then save to your account is 'locked up' by the encryption key while still on your computer, then sent in encrypted form to LastPass' server.

2. The sensitive data that is harbored on our servers is always encrypted before it's sent to us, so all we receive is gibberish.

Since the encryption key is locally created each time you submit your MP and email, all that we store and have access to on our servers is your encrypted data. Without your unique encryption key, your sensitive data is meaningless gibberish. Even if someone were to mandate that we provide a copy of our database, the data would still be unreadable without your encryption key.

3. We never receive the key to decrypt that data.

The unique encryption key formed from the hashing of your email and MP is never sent to our servers. We never, for any reason, would ask you for your MP, so the key remains safely with you.

Source: *http://blog.lastpass.com/2010/07/lastpass-gets-green-light-from-security.html*

Because of the fact that they never have access to your Lastpass master password that decrypts all your data, if you lose that password, all your data is truly irretrievable. There is no password reset function. You are the only one with that password and it is your responsibility to both remember it and keep it a secret.

Anytime you use a service or piece of software created or run by a third-party, there is some leap of faith, but this service has been vetted by someone that I personally trust in the cyber-security arena, Steve Gibson. Feel free to read this transcript (*https://www.grc.com/sn/sn-256.htm*) of the podcast in which he describes his research into Lastpass.

Personally, I have been using Lastpass to organize, create, and keep track of my passwords for more than five years now and I don't want to think about what a pain it would be to keep track of usernames, passwords, and profiles without it.

Sharing Passwords

There are inevitable circumstances where you will have to share login credentials with third-parties. A family member, an employee, or contractor may need to access your account to complete a particular task. You don't want to give them the actual password itself, but Lastpass allows you to share the ability to log into a particular account without actually revealing the specific password.

The recipient has to have both a Lastpass account and the browser extension installed in order to use the login credentials that you shared with them.

Logging Yourself Out

If you have a super-secure password, yet never log yourself out, nobody that has access to your computer or phone will even need that password. I know it seems convenient to remain logged in all the time and have your main passwords autofill, but those extra few seconds spend typing your password each time buy you quite a bit of extra security.

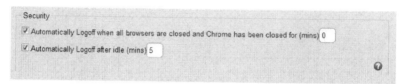

Wherever possible, don't have your programs automatically remember login information like usernames and passwords:

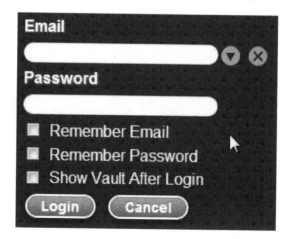

Writing Passwords Down

Recently, UK security personnel detained a man carrying encrypted hard drives full of extremely sensitive leaked documents. When they detained this courier, he had with him a piece of paper with the password written on it.

I understand the dilemma of wanting a complicated password that would be difficult to brute-force, but then having difficulty remembering it. We have all written down passwords at some time, but you need to take steps to make it less dangerous. You should alter the password in some way. You can come up with your own personal method, but some ideas would be:

- Memorize and don't write down the first or last few characters

- Insert random letters every 1, 2, or 3 digits

- Split the password in the middle and write the last half first

- Write the password backwards

- Any combination of the above

This way, you don't have to remember the entire password. You only have to remember your secret pattern to rearrange it.

Private Communications

Email

Most of us, me included, have reputable looking email addresses with recognizable major internet companies like Google, Microsoft, Yahoo, or others. These webmail services offer a number of leading edge functionalities that allow us to search our email with ease and access it quickly and easily from a number of different devices. Unfortunately, high security is not one of the features of these accounts. It has been revealed in recently released documents that the United States government has not only been tapping into the data streams coming into and going out of these companies, but also secretly coercing them to provide information that will allow them to decipher and gain access to all that information, even without a warrant.

Many people see this as a problem and wisely seek out more secure solutions. In the wake of recent revelations, some companies are attempting to capitalize on the current events by advertising their services as private and secure without really explaining what that means. If you do a search for "secure email", "private email", or "encrypted email" you will find a number of services that make lofty claims concerning the privacy of your email, but in reality, most of them only encrypt your data while it is at rest.

Please don't misunderstand me. This is better than most webmail service providers. If someone comes in and happens to steal a hard drive from the server that is storing your personal email, they will have a difficult time accessing that data because it was encrypted before it was stored.

Unfortunately, with this system, the encrypting and decrypting password is still transmitted over the internet and all the encryption work is all done on a distant server. This means that after your email is decrypted, it is transmitted to you in plaintext. If your email is intercepted at any point during transit, it is unencrypted and much more easily accessed.

The key to private email communication is ensuring that the encryption is end-to-end. In a perfect world, we could read encrypted text and our brain would be the only thing able to decrypt it, but unless you're some kind of savant, you will need to rely on computer processing power to do the encryption and decryption on your brain's behalf. In that case, the least we should do is make sure that the initial encryption and the final decryption happen as close to the sender and recipient as possible.

We don't want the encryption work being done on a distant server and a plaintext email being transmitted to us. We want the encryption and decryption to happen on our own computer with a key and password that only we know. In this case, if our email is intercepted at any point along the way, even while on the email provider's servers, only gibberish will be revealed. The message will not be decrypted and rendered in plain text until it is on our computer and your key and password are provided.

PGP Encryption

While I don't claim to understand the mathematical details behind exactly why PGP encryption works, I will do my best to explain how it works with sweeping generalities. The encryption is accomplished by means of a pair of keys that are generated based on a passphrase or password. This pair of keys is comprised of a public key and a private key. The public key is meant to be published for others to use when sending you a message. A message that is encrypted using your public key can only be decrypted using your private key and password.

Before anyone sends you a PGP encrypted email, they must first have your public key. For this reason, it is advantageous for you to make this public key widely available. Likewise, for you to respond to the email with your own encrypted correspondence, you must have the other person's public key.

The great part of this system is that at no time does a password or secret key have to be transmitted over the internet.

One "problem" with the system is the difficulty in verifying who a public key truly belongs to. I can generate a public key and attach it to any name I choose. For this reason, you should only use keys from a source you trust.

Webmail vs. Local Email Client

People access their email in many different ways. The two most common ways to access and use email are via a web interface or a locally installed email client. We will look at two specific examples of these different ways of accessing email and show you how to use PGP encryption for your email in either situation.

The key to all this is Pre-Internet Encryption (PIE). The message should be encrypted before it ever leaves your machine. All the encryption and decryption should happen on your machine so that the unencrypted message is never out on the internet. We will look at how to do this on Thunderbird with the Enigmail add-on as well as with Chrome and the extension Mailvelope for webmail.

Chrome and Mailvelope for Webmail

Mailvelope (*http://www.mailvelope.com/*) is a Chrome add-on that offers end-to-end encryption and allows you to encrypt and decrypt your email in a web interface directly from the browser. Your encryption keys are only stored on your computer and never sent out over the internet. Your password is only kept by you and cannot be stored by the add-on or browser for longer than a single session. It is a bit annoying that Lastpass is not able to autofill the encryption passphrase/password, but a simple copy and paste will do the job.

With Mailvelope, you write out your email in the regular "compose" window. When you are finished, you click a little superimposed button in the upper-right corner that allows you to select the specific key you want to use to encrypt the email. The add-on then automatically replaces the plaintext that you had typed into the compose window with the new, post-encryption ciphertext. Decrypting received email is just as simple. You select the appropriate key for decryption, put in the password, and the add-on does the rest.

The add-on also has a simple interface for importing, exporting, generating and managing PGP keys. You can find detailed tutorials with screenshots for installing, setting up, and using the add-on here: *http://www.mailvelope.com/help*.

Thunderbird and Enigmail

When it comes to using PGP encryption in combination with a desktop email client, I recommend Mozilla Thunderbird (*http://www.mozilla.org/en-US/thunderbird/*) and the Enigmail extension (*https://www.enigmail.net/home/index.php*). They work in combination with another desktop application, GnuPG (*http://www.gnupg.org/download/*). GnuPG runs in the background and allows you to simply and easily encrypt and decrypt messages that you send and receive in the Thunderbird email client.

THE ENIGMAIL PROJECT
OPENPGP EMAIL SECURITY FOR MOZILLA APPLICATIONS

Here is a Thunderbird install guide for Windows:
https://support.mozillamessaging.com/en-US/kb/installing-thunderbird-windows?s=install&as=s

Here is documentation for installing, setting up, and using Enigmail with Thunderbird and GnuPG
https://www.enigmail.net/documentation/quickstart.php

Desktop Client

If you just want an unaffiliated desktop app to manage and sign keys and encrypt and decrypt messages and files, you need look no further than GPG4Win (_http://www.gpg4win.org/_). This fully featured program and all of its components are entirely free and open source. As you might have already inferred from the name, this is a Windows application.

Check out the features here:
http://www.gpg4win.org/features.html.

User documentation is available in the form of a PDF document that can be downloaded here:
http://www.gpg4win.org/documentation.html

Web Interface for PGP Encryption

If you don't want to install any software or extensions, iGolder (_http://www.igolder.com/pgp/_) offers a web interface to generate keys (_http://www.igolder.com/pgp/generate-key/_), encode (_http://www.igolder.com/pgp/encryption/_), and decode messages (_http://www.igolder.com/pgp/decryption/_). They state that "iGolder respects your privacy and does not log _or_ monitor any activity (encryption) done on this web page." There is obviously a little more trust involved and a lot more copying and pasting, but it could be an option for a situation where you aren't able to run software on the machine you are using.

Publishing a public key

In order for your public encryption key to be useful, it should be widely published and easily available. Anyone who wants to reach you in a secure manner should be able to quickly and easily access your public key. You can get creative in the ways that you share your key, but the obvious methods are including it in your email signature and on your personal and professional websites.

In your email signature, you can either include the text of the key itself or a link to the key file stored on a server somewhere for people to access. On your website, you have the same choice. You can include the full text of the key on a webpage or you can simply include a direct link to download the key file. I recommend that you keep the link as short as possible and make it easy to remember. This way, you can share it verbally and people can access the key file without having to write down a long and convoluted URL.

It is also a good idea to include a link to instructions for using a PGP key file for people that may see the link and want to use more secure communications, but don't know how.

Email Text Steganography

ste·ga·no·graph·y
/ˌstegəˈnägrəfi/

noun

1. the practice of concealing messages or information within other nonsecret text or data.

According to recently leaked documents, the NSA stores all encrypted messages forever (*http://www.technewsworld.com/ story/79117.html*) in case a new technology arrives that allows them to decrypt them in the future, but what if they didn't know that the email even contained an encrypted message? What if the message didn't look like high-security encrypted communications, but rather the delusional rant of a Nigerian scammer?

Spammimic (*http://www.spammimic.com/*) allows you to hide your message in innocuous sounding spam that nobody wants to bother with. You can take a message encrypted via PGP:

```
-----BEGIN PGP MESSAGE-----
Version: OpenPGP.js v.1.20130820
Comment: http://openpgpjs.org
```

wcFMA628KEA5Vno7ARAAvYCOV/0jxbKv5I0gpUksVlpc8wrTTwM8D+S7e4jA
Pg5MCHlGHBgs0TOFXYWlLYpstmoQ+xrt5NXQgxlPVTSFuf7O4E4NHpmBmsmU
QC28L3D829xfl5H9ks0FNFsYSqlLJW2FQQ5f4wDd6sHmfrMMkfB747+g03bY
EDvG+BBSSU1WbWJSG0mbKSm255ACqiBcNupj0DQgrzlzF5SDlGhCk3g/SNpq
2Qn3JjqKBX39D8LPByUCAswsUiQr9Rp0NMroi9ZgSmM/gSqVZSHuHNTvSwad
ff/UqTEZMipdeFgvB7KYjZu9BSXkNu/QgXlo0Mw4LFb2+snS7GzXDT1VlFud
G1ia/CRP9LI/I4y5FmNTGNAP9N0gBVPGhUSFfOigMjdAh9gYssTmKX83Fr+T
3u6cB+xzqxgneCXhsGUkllB4zdgLgO58Vw+FZcbfEKehOXA6vxwm7IR8wOBS

Paste it into the site's encoder:

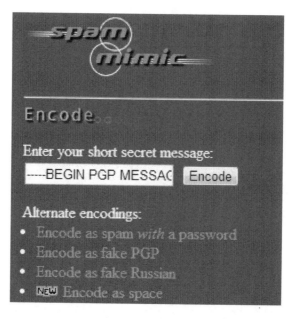

And it will come out looking like a rambling spam email:

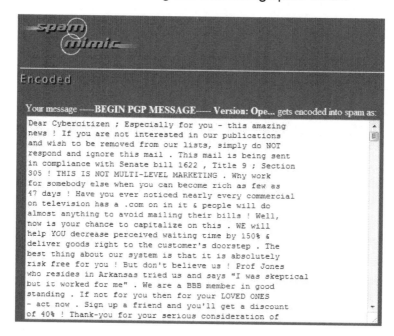

When the recipient receives the email, they can decode it on the website by pasting the message into the decoding utility:

Decode

Paste in a spam-encoded message:

```
forever if you don't order now . Sign up a friend and
your friend will be rich too ! Best regards . Dear
Friend , This letter was specially selected to be sent
to you . If you are not interested in our publications
and wish to be removed from our lists, simply do NOT
respond and ignore this mail . This mail is being sent
in compliance with Senate bill 2416 , Title 8 ; Section
302 ! This is NOT unsolicited bulk mail ! Why work
for somebody else when you can become rich within 72
weeks . Have you ever noticed nearly every commercial
on television has a .com on in it & the baby boomers
are more demanding than their parents . Well, now is
your chance to capitalize on this . We will help you
turn your business into an E-BUSINESS & deliver goods
right to the customer's doorstep . You can begin at
absolutely no cost to you . But don't believe us !
Ms Anderson of Indiana tried us and says "Now I'm rich,
Rich, RICH" ! This offer is 100% legal ! If not for
you then for your loved ones - act now ! Sign up a
friend and you get half off . Thanks .
```

Decode

After decoding the original message is revealed:

Decoded

Your spam message **Dear Cybercitizen ; Especially for you -...** decodes to:

----BEGIN PGP MESSAG   Encode

Let me reiterate that this service provides no real security and you should not rely solely on this service for encryption. There are no passwords. Anyone can paste the fake spam email into the decoder and find out what the original message said. This service only offers ubiquity. It theoretically allows your emails to blend into the massive horde of spam that travels through the internet. The real question is: How many of the messages sitting in your spam folder are actually secret messages that you need to read?

Private Email Attachments

Encryption

Mailvelope only encrypts the text of a message, not email attachments. If you want to send encrypted attachments, you will need to encrypt the file before attaching it to the email. You can use a free program like 7-Zip (*http://www.7-zip.org/*) to create a password protected .zip or .rar file with 256-AES Encryption.

You could include the password in the encrypted text of the email so that when the recipient decrypts the message, they can then decrypt the attached file.

Steganography

We briefly discussed steganography when it comes to email text, but there are many other applications for steganography. In this case, we are looking for ways to keep your private attachment from prying eyes.

If your file is truly sensitive, you should encrypt the file first. Steganography is merely hiding something and should not to be confused with real encryption. Once your sensitive file is encrypted, we can hide it in a file or group of files to be retrieved later.

OpenPuff
(_http://embeddedsw.net/OpenPuff_Steganography_Home.html_)
is a steganography tool that can both encrypt and hide your private files in a variety of different types of files.

- Images (BMP, JPG, PCX, PNG, TGA)

- Audio support (AIFF, MP3, NEXT/SUN, WAV)

- Video support (3GP, MP4, MPG, VOB)

- Flash-Adobe support (FLV, SWF, PDF)

This allows you to use as a carrier, whatever type of file you think would seem most inconspicuous. If you are sending a file to a podcaster or radio journalist, stick it in a large WAV file. If you are sending it to a family member or friend, stick the file in a photo of your cute kids. To a developer or businessman, maybe use an FLV or PDF file. You have quite a selection to choose from.

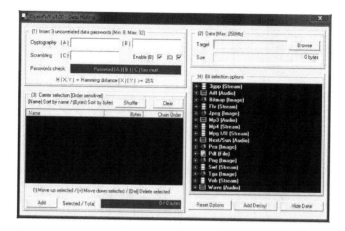

To hide data, you choose three passwords, select a carrier file (the file that everyone sees), and select the data that needs to be hidden. OpenPuff does its work, then you can attach the carrier file to your email and send it.

In order to "unhide" the private data, the party receiving the hidden file will also need to have OpenPuff and the 3 passwords you used.

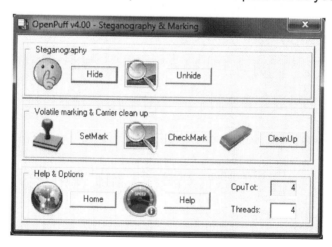

While OpenPuff is my go-to steganography tool because of its simplicity and versatility, there are quite a few tools out there if you are looking for a specific feature that OpenPuff may not have. Here is a steganography software list:
http://www.jjtc.com/Steganography/tools.html

Email Tracking

If you have ever used an email newsletter service like Aweber or Mailchimp, you know that they can provide an amazing amount of detail about which recipients have opened your email newsletters and exactly which links have been clicked. This tracking isn't limited to newsletters and big analytics suites.

Even nosy individuals can use free tools like SpyPig (*http://www.spypig.com/*) to insert images into their email that, when downloaded by your email client, will notify the sender that you have opened their email. If several days go by with no response, the recipient may receive another email wondering what is taking them so long.

If you want to keep your email truly private and make sure that people won't be able to spy and find out if you have opened their email, you need to make sure that your email client or service is not automatically downloading "external content". External content is in quite a bit of email and without it, many newsletters and sales advertisements look like jumbled lots of text.

Images are not displayed. Display images below - Always display images from do_r

By default, Mozilla Thunderbird blocks all external content (*http://kb.mozillazine.org/Privacy_basics_(Thunderbird)*). Gmail blocks it by default from "unknown" senders (*http://email.about.com/od/gmailtips/qt/Have_Gmail_Display_Re mote_Images_for_Trusted_Senders.htm*). If you have emailed somebody twice, they consider them to be a trusted contact and automatically display the html images, etc. You can change this in the "General" tab of the settings so that it will always ask before displaying external content.

External content: ○ Always display external content (such as images) sent by trusted senders - Learn more
              ● Ask before displaying external content

Keeping them from tracking your clicked links is a bit more challenging. The best method to avoid link tracking is to do your own separate search to find and access the content.

Chat

Chat falls somewhere in between direct voice communication and email. You can communicate back and forth in close to real time, yet the bandwidth requirement is relatively low because you are only transmitting and receiving text.

For text chatting, I recommend CryptoCat (*https://crypto.cat/*). Here is a basic explanation from their website:

> *Cryptocat is free software that aims to provide an open, accessible Instant Messaging environment that encrypts your conversations and works right in your browser. Cryptocat is an open source experiment — the goal is to provide the easiest, most accessible way to chat while maintaining your privacy online, because privacy needs to be accessible*

CryptoCat has a collection of browser apps for Chrome (*https://chrome.google.com/webstore/detail/gonbigodpnfghidm nphnadhepmbabhij*), Firefox (*https://addons.mozilla.org/en-US/firefox/addon/cryptocat/*), and Safari (*https://crypto.cat/get/cryptocat.safariextz*) as well as a Mac client (*https://itunes.apple.com/us/app/cryptocat/id613116229?ls=1& mt=12*). You will need to install the app in your browser. There are download links on their main page for each of the different browsers.

While the CryptoCat interface won't be winning any awards for beauty, it is simple and useable.

To access the chat area, you need only enter a "conversation name" and a nickname.

There is no password protection. The other chat parties only need to know the conversation name to access the chat area to converse with you. CryptoCat is simple, but does a great job at what it does.

Remember that CryptoCat only encrypts your communications and does nothing to anonymize you. You should use TOR or an off-site internet connection to help with anonymity.

Voice Communications

Everyone knows how to use Skype, but it is notoriously insecure with built-in backdoors for the NSA that could be potentially used by any hacker. According to recently leaked documents (*http://news.cnet.com/8301-13578_3-57593339-38/nsa-docs-boast-now-we-can-wiretap-skype-video-calls/*), the NSA claims to have "direct access" to Skype for their PRISM program.

If Skype is out, what is available for secure voice communications? We have discussed how to encrypt email communications, but what about when you want to have a quick conversation without using your keyboard?

One options that seems to have many people filled with anticipation is Tox.im (*http://tox.im/*), a free and open source software solution that despite appearing to have a beautiful interface, has not been released yet.

Another option that is actually available is a client offering end-to-end encrypted voice calls via several services and protocols called Jitsi:

Jitsi (formerly SIP Communicator) is an audio/video and chat communicator that supports protocols such as SIP, XMPP/Jabber, AIM/ICQ, Windows Live, and Yahoo!.

If you don't already have an SIP account to use with Jitsi, you can sign up for free here:
https://www.ippi.fr/index.php?page=home&lang=44&lang=44

with a simple signup that does require one-time email address verification(see the section on email verification for dealing with this).

Here is a list of the Jitsi features: *https://jitsi.org/Main/Features* and here is documentation with screenshots for setting it up: *https://jitsi.org/Documentation/UserDocumentation*

You can read more about the security here: *https://jitsi.org/index.php/Documentation/ZrtpFAQ*

If you are looking for something to make your mobile phone calls more secure, you should check out the android app Redphone for Mobile (*https://play.google.com/store/apps/details?id= org.thoughtcrime.redphone&hl=en*) . The app integrates with the dialer to create a seamless experience. If the person you are attempting to call also has Redphone installed, it automatically offers you the option to use Redphone to make an encrypted call via the data connection. It may not be perfect security-wise, but it certainly beats making normal, unsecured voice calls via cellular networks. You can read more about the vulnerabilities of typical mobile phone communications in "Is My Cell Phone Bugged?" (*http://www.amazon.com/gp/product/B0052Z8FK0/ persoarmampod-20*)

Encrypted Data

Encrypted communications are great, but what about the stuff on your hard drive? What if someone gains access to your hard drives full of stored personal data? While hardware access or stored data access is not as likely as someone accessing your communications, it is still a threat that requires preparation. With proper data encryption and backup, you shouldn't have to worry about your data being compromised if your hardware is stolen or accessed.

Local Storage

When it comes to encrypting your stored data, there are a number of options, but TrueCrypt (*http://www.truecrypt.org/*) stands head and shoulders above the rest. It isn't the simplest program out there, but the options and features are amazing.

- Creates a virtual encrypted disk within a file and mounts it as a real disk.

- Encrypts an entire partition or storage device such as USB flash drive or hard drive.

- Encrypts a partition or drive where Windows is installed (pre-boot authentication).

- Creates hidden volumes (steganography) and hidden operating systems that provide plausible deniability, in case an adversary forces you to reveal the password.

Start with encrypting your boot drive or partition. This can be done at any time and does not require you to do a new operating system install. This will require a password to decrypt your partition before the computer can even boot. Here are instructions for encrypting your boot partition:
http://www.truecrypt.org/docs/system-encryption

If you want to take it a step further, you can set up a hidden operating system. This will allow you to boot to one operating system with one password and another hidden operating system with another password. The setup for a hidden operating system is a little more complicated and does require a fresh operating system install. Here are the detailed instructions and caveats:
http://www.truecrypt.org/docs/hidden-operating-system

You can do essentially the same thing when it comes to non-boot storage. You can create encrypted volumes that no one can even see or know about unless you provide a specific password to mount that volume. Here are instructions for setting up hidden volumes:
http://www.truecrypt.org/hiddenvolume

TrueCrypt (*http://www.truecrypt.org/*) is a powerful free and open-source program that can meet nearly all your data encryption needs.

Cloud Storage and Backup

Cloud storage is convenient for a number of reasons, but having your personal data on remote servers can make it quite vulnerable. Fortunately, there are options for you to securely synchronize and store data remotely whether it be on your own servers or someone else's. We will discuss your options for securing your Dropbox files as well as a DIY BitTorrent solution that may surprise you.

Dropbox

Technically, you can open a free account with an unlinked and anonymous email address and only use the limited amount of space. This would never require you to provide payment information and you could remain anonymous. Unfortunately, the beauty of Dropbox.com is its ubiquity and the ability to access it from anywhere and use it connected to a variety of services. This is very difficult to do in a truly anonymous manner. For that reason, we won't focus on keeping it anonymous, but rather how to encrypt the data you store on it.

There are several options for securing your data for storage on Dropbox servers. The key to each of these solutions is encrypting the data before it leaves your computer. All the software and services mentioned below encrypt the data on your computer so that only encrypted data is transmitted and stored on Dropbox servers. If Dropbox is ever compromised, your data is still secure because you encrypted it before sharing with Dropbox.

Encrypt individual files

If you only have a few files that you want to encrypt and store in the cloud, you may find that encrypting those few files individually is your best option.

You can use a free program like 7-Zip (*http://www.7-zip.org/*) to create a password protected .zip or .rar file with 256-AES Encryption.

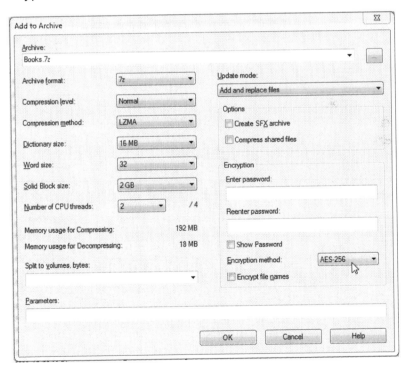

Use a third-party automatic encryption program

Several enterprising individuals have recognized the need for a simple system for encrypting Dropbox data before it heads off into the cloud. I have tested three of these applications: BoxCryptor (*https://www.boxcryptor.com/*), Viivo (*http://www.viivo.com/*), and Cloudfogger (*http://www.cloudfogger.com/en/*). They vary slightly in minor features, but all create a subfolder in your Dropbox folder to store encrypted data. They then create a different folder elsewhere on your computer where you access your data in its unencrypted form. As you access and change data in that folder, the program works in the background to re-encrypt and update the data in the actual Dropbox folder.

These services can be setup so that your password is never transmitted over the internet or stored anywhere other than on your computer. All the encryption is done on your computer by these apps.

These programs also have mobile apps that will allow you to access the encrypted files from your smartphone.

Truecrypt container

If you want to use an open source solution, TrueCrypt (*http://www.truecrypt.org/*) can do something similar to these apps like BoxCryptor, Viivo, and Cloudfogger. There is a little more manual setup involved, but it ends up doing basically the same thing. It stores your encrypted data in your Dropbox folder, while providing access to the un-encrypted data in a different location.

To do this, you need to create a Truecrypt volume and place it in your Dropbox folder. You will need to determine the size of the volume in advance. There are several considerations when it comes to determining the size of your Truecrypt volume. First, it should be smaller than the available Dropbox space. Second, your volume will initially need to be uploaded in its entirety to Dropbox. If you have a slow internet connection, you may not want to create a 10 GB volume. You may want to create several smaller volumes as you need more space. Finally, you need to consider the size of the files you want to encrypt and store so that you create a volume large enough to store them all.

Once the volume is finished with the initial upload to Dropbox, it will not be entirely refreshed as you change and update the individual files within it. Only the changed portions of the volume that correspond with the individual changed files will be re-uploaded to Dropbox.

Once you create the Truecrypt volume, you can mount it so that it appears as drive in your file explorer programs. This allows you to easily access the storage space and unencrypted files within.

Here is a tutorial for setting up a Truecrypt volume:
http://www.truecrypt.org/docs/tutorial

BitTorrent Sync

Whenever I need to download a large file, I prefer to download it via BitTorrent. This allows me to pause and restart without cancelling the download and having to start over again later. I can also achieve some very high download speeds. BitTorrent Labs (*http://labs.bittorrent.com/experiments/sync.html/*) recently released BitTorrent Sync software that uses the BitTorrent protocol to synchronize your data. You can use this program to synchronize your data to a NAS device on a local network, a remote server, or a NAS device at a friend's house. The system is currently still in beta, but it is surprisingly flexible and robust.

This could be considered a competitor to Dropbox, but it is important to realize that your devices will synchronize directly with each other. Your data does not go to a cloud server, then back down to your device. Your devices connect directly to exchange data. While the software is not open source, it is completely independent and does not "phone home" or share your data. I won't get into the technical details, but it does receive the endorsement of security guru, Steve Gibson. You can read about his analysis here: *https://www.grc.com/sn/sn-402.txt*

BitTorrent Sync is currently compatible with a number of devices:

Windows
(XP SP3 or newer)

Mac OSX
(10.6 or newer)

Mobile:

Android

iOS

Linux and NAS Devices:

- Linux ARM
- Linux PowerPC
- Linux i386
- Linux x64
- Linux PPC QorIQ

- Linux_i386 (glibc 2.3)
- Linux_x64 (glibc 2.3)
- FreeBSD i386
- FreeBSD X64

If you sit down and think for a few minutes, you can find of a number of ways to use this software for synchronizing and backing up your files and data across desktop devices, NAS devices, and mobile devices. I see this as particularly useful for synchronizing data from my mobile phone. If I want to move photos or data to my desktop computer, there is no real need to use the cloud as a go-between.

The primary use for this BitTorrent Sync is backing up your data. With a robust feature set including end-to-end encryption, this looks to be a great choice.

If you want off-site backup, you could exchange NAS devices with a trustworthy friend and have BitTorrent Sync take care of the synchronization. If all your data is already encrypted and you don't mind storing it on a server owned by someone else, you could run BitTorrent Sync on a Virtual Private Server for your own "cloud" service.

Bittorrent Sync
http://labs.bittorrent.com/experiments/sync.html

BitTorrent Sync FAQs
http://forum.bittorrent.com/topic/16410-bittorrent-sync-faq/

BitTorrent Sync Setup
http://labs.bittorrent.com/experiments/sync/get-started.html

Android App
https://play.google.com/store/apps/details?id=com.bittorrent.sync

BitTorrent Sync and FreeNas
http://blog.bittorrent.com/2013/06/17/bittorrent-sync-turning-your-old-computer-into-an-nas-drive/

Titanium Backup for Android

While Titanium Backup (*https://play.google.com/store/apps/ details?id=com.keramidas.TitaniumBackup*) is only available for Android users with rooted phones, the app is so powerful and useful that I feel I would be remiss not to mention it. Titanium Backup allows you complete, granular control when it comes to the backup of your phone. You can backup your phone settings as well as individual apps and their data. You can restore individual apps and their data that you may have accidentally messed up or you can restore every app and make your phone exactly how it was before it was broken or wiped. I can attest that the restore process is quite simple, even when dealing with a completely new phone.

Titanium Backup supports backing up your data to several different cloud services and also offers you the option to encrypt the data before sending it out for storage. The encryption password never leaves your device and is not stored elsewhere in case you forget it.

There are many more features than I have the time to discuss here. Suffice it to say that if you have a rooted Android device, you should be using Titanium Backup. Here is their official site with loads of information:
http://matrixrewriter.com/android/

Anonymous Financial Transactions

Do you want to purchase hosting anonymously so that your revolutionary blog posts won't be linked back to the real you via your real-life banking information? Do you want to make online donations to a radical cause without it being traced back to you? Do you want additional Dropbox storage without connecting the account to your real identity? Do you want to purchase VPN service or a subscription to any other security service without linking back to your real identity?

Then pay attention!

Anonymous financial transactions on the internet are possible, but due to copious new banking regulations in recent years, it can be a pain. The traveling to purchase and pick up prepaid charge cards in person is a hassle. The extra fees are annoying. Figuring out expiration dates and reading the fine print can be a nuisance, but what is your anonymity worth?

When we talk about anonymity concerning financial transactions, we mean that there should be no trail or connection to your real identity. This is almost impossible when it comes to receiving money. No one wants to hand cash to an anonymous person. I can't offer you advice for anonymously monetizing your internet empire, but I can offer you possible solutions for making online purchases anonymously.

Truly Anonymous Credit Cards

We have already discussed our definition of anonymity for this book. If we are required to provide actual, personally identifiable information like social security numbers, dates of birth, personal phone numbers, and home addresses, there is no real anonymity. The purchases can be linked to the real you.

You will see numerous prepaid cards at your various local retail institutions, but the majority of them will ask you for personally identifiable information and verify that information. There are legal reasons for this. Section 326 of the Patriot Act (*http://en.wikipedia.org/wiki/Patriot_Act,_Title_III,_Subtitle_A#Sec. _326._Verification_of_identification*) requires financial institutions to collect and verify your ID when you open an "account." If you look closely at the fine print, you will find disclaimers along these lines:

> The USA PATRIOT Act is a Federal law that requires all financial institutions to obtain, verify, and record information that identifies each person who opens an account. You will be asked to provide your name, address, date of birth, and other information that will allow us to identify you. You may also be asked to provide documentation as proof of identification.

Don't worry, I didn't drag you through all this information just to tell you what isn't possible. There are some exceptions that haven't been brought under the rules of Section 326 yet. I'm talking about the very uninteresting-sounding gift cards. Who ever heard of James Bond busting out a gift card to make anonymous purchases when he was being hunted by the law? So un-cool!

They may not be cool, but they get the job done in many situations without requiring you to forfeit your precious personally identifiable information. Sure, they have their drawbacks. Many cannot be recharged, carry balances above $500, or be used by certain retailers because they may not offer address verification system checks, but anonymity comes with its limitations.

The card that I will recommend here is associated with Simon Malls (*https://www.simon.com/giftcard/*), can be bought in person with cash, and charged initially with any denomination up to $500. There is a one-time fee of $2 when you purchase the card and it cannot be reloaded. When you register the card online, you should do so from a proxy and use a fictional address that you have stored in Lastpass. If an online retailer requires an address for verification, you can provide the fictional one that you used at registration. Use this page: *http://www.simon.com/search* to search for the nearest location where you can purchase a Simon Gift Card.

As with most non-rechargeable gift cards, you may end up with a small, practically unusable balance on the card as it nears the end of its life. Please consider donating that balance to a rights and advocacy organization or a charity of your choosing.

Skimmers

While it wouldn't compromise your real identity with one of the cards mentioned above, skimmers are nefarious devices that are laid over credit card scanners in a concealed manner to "skim" your credit card information as you use it at an ATM, gas station, or other device used to legally scan a credit card.

Scammers are becoming quite adept at affixing these devices in a manner that looks above-board and raises little suspicion. Typical devices at an ATM would have two parts: A device to read the magnetic strip as you insert your card and a thin keypad laid over the ATM keypad to get your PIN.

The best defense against these devices is to look for anything that looks "fishy". Are there protruding edges? Does the scanner look like it sticks out a little too far? Do you see any abnormally large seams or gaps? If so, find a different ATM.

You can find more information and photos of skimmers here: *http://krebsonsecurity.com/all-about-skimmers/*. If you want to see how skilled and creatively concealed these skimmers can really be, check out this YouTube video: *http://youtu.be/R_3LIYgPlZc*

Bitcoin

I'm sure that most people reading this book thought I was headed straight for Bitcoin when we entered the Anonymous Financial Transactions section, but it has enough drawbacks to be relegated to 2nd place on the list. While I love the concept of Bitcoin, it still falls short when it comes to cashing in and exchanging your Bitcoins for your local currency. Somewhere in that process, you have to connect and transfer to a bank account with your real, verified information. The same thing goes for putting your money into the Bitcoin ecosystem. You can't purchase Bitcoins with cash at your local Walmart yet. When you make Bitcoin purchase, the money comes from somewhere and that is *usually* a bank account with your personally identifiable information attached.

That being said, there are ways to acquire Bitcoins without purchasing them via electronic bank transfer. You can sell items, accept Bitcoin payments, and build up a balance. You can purchase Bitcoins in a face-to-face transaction with a friend or complete stranger who wants to cash out in an anonymous manner without using a typical currency exchange service. You can "mine" them.

Even if the Bitcoins are acquired in an untraceable manner, there is the fact that the Bitcoin collects information with each transaction that it is used for. Bitcoins are pseudonymous, not anonymous like most people believe. The jury is still out as to the practical realities of the usefulness of the collected information when it comes to tracing that back to a real live human being.

Every Bitcoin has a "block chain" (*https://en.bitcoin.it/wiki/Block_chain*) that records the address of every wallet that has held it. Every transaction adds another wallet address to the list. The IP addresses of every transaction are publicly available (*http://blockchain.info/*). The real question is whether or not you can effectively keep your Bitcoin wallet address from being connected to the real you. This is theoretically possible, but you have to be very careful.

Creating an Anonymous Bitcoin Wallet

Although tedious, you can create a truly anonymous Bitcoin wallet and use it to make anonymous online purchases. Here is the process:

To start with a truly clean slate, purchase an inexpensive laptop computer. It doesn't need to be new or fast. It should have a wifi connection and a useable CD drive, SD card slot, or USB port to boot from. Feel free to remove the hard drive. We will be using a bootable Linux Live CD and you won't need it. I recommend the simple and well-known TAILS (The Amnesiac Incognito Live System) *https://tails.boum.org/*. Download TAILS and burn it to a CD or place it on a USB stick or SD card. TAILS is preconfigured to protect your anonymity, use TOR, and leave no trace.

For an extra security buffer, do not use your home internet connection. Your home internet connection is linked to your real identity because of your payment information on file with your ISP. If you make any mistakes, this way, the penalty is not accidentally revealing your real IP address.

From a free wifi hotspot that doesn't require registration, use TAILS to connect to the internet. When you connect, verify that your IP address is actually being masked (*https://check.torproject.org/*) and check your IP address for DNS leaks (*https://www.dnsleaktest.com/*). If everything checks out, it is now time to create your anonymous wallet.

Download: *http://bitaddress.org.html/*

After the file is finished downloading, disconnect from the internet, disable wifi, etc. Now, open the file in your browser and it will generate a wallet address. You should write down or record the wallet address and the private key somewhere safe.

Funding an Anonymous Bitcoin Wallet

Now that you have an anonymous bitcoin wallet, you need to fund it or put some bitcoin in it. Do **NOT** use a traditional bitcoin exchange like Mt. Gox (*https://www.mtgox.com/*) or you will end up associating your personal banking information with this bitcoin wallet and connecting it to your real identity.

You can use a service like ZipZap (*http://www.zipzapinc.com/*) to make a cash payment at a local business to purchase Bitcoins for your new, anonymous wallet. Make sure that you only access the site from an off-site internet connection via Tor and provide only information that cannot be linked back to you, including a truly anonymous email address. You should probably create a new email address for each deposit so that they aren't associated in a way that can create patterns for investigators.

Another option for funding your anonymous bitcoin wallet would be Localbitcoins (*https://localbitcoins.com/instant-bitcoins/*) . This service helps to connect you with local individuals who are looking to buy or sell their Bitcoins. You can search for individuals who want to make cash transactions in your area. I was able to find several local sellers looking for cash transactions, even here in Nepal.

Spending Bitcoins Anonymously

Using TAILS again from an off-site internet connection, download Electrum (*http://electrum.org/*). Because you are working from a live CD that will leave no trace, you will have to re-download each time you do this. You will use Electrum to access your bitcoin wallet.

Technically, you should be good to go ahead and spend your Bitcoins using the wallet you already created, but you might want to go a step further to make sure that your various purchases and transactions won't be linked together because you made all the purchases from the same wallet.

To prevent this, we are going to use a Bitcoin mixing service to disconnect our main storage wallet from our "spending wallets" that we are going to use to make actual purchases down the road. For maximum anonymity, you should do the bitcoin mixing process several times.

To understand bitcoin mixing/sharing (*https://blockchain.info/ wallet/send-shared*), imagine several strangers with different bills. For the sake of anonymity, you and the other strangers agree to deposit the money for these bills in the same account and use that account to pay each of the bills. The mixing service that matches up these strangers takes a small cut (~.5%) and dumps all the records after a maximum of 8 hours.

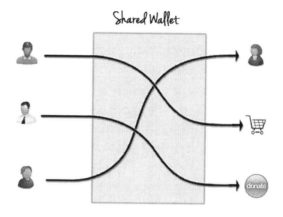

Shared Wallet

Because Bitcoins record the address of every wallet that they are held by, and people can look at the location history of every Bitcoin, the illustration would be even more detailed if we pretended that each of the strangers contributed marked bills to the pool and withdrew someone else's marked bills to pay for their transactions. In other words, you could end up using Bitcoins to make your purchase that someone else acquired by nefarious means. You never know.

Up to this point, your wallet's address and key have never been transmitted over the internet. As we start to share this data for mixing and purchases, we want to obscure our real IP address, but we don't want to use TOR because the exit nodes can be easily monitored to intercept your wallet information. The best option at this point would be a VPN service, particularly one that can be purchased with Bitcoins.

I know, I know. How do you make a protected and anonymous transaction to purchase the VPN service without already having the VPN service? You will have to take a risk when you make that first purchase of the VPN service. You should still follow this process and use a mixing wallet, but also bear in mind that there is some extra risk while making that VPN purchase.

Using the process outlined above, you can create numerous Bitcoin wallets to temporarily hold your Bitcoins as you move them around from one mixing service to another. Never use one of these temporary "mixing wallets" more than once. After you feel that you have done enough mixing, you should have the bitcoins end up in a completely different "spending wallet." This is the wallet that will actually give the Bitcoins to the merchant or merchants that you transact with.

After all the mixing, your spending wallet is now disconnected from your primary wallet that holds the majority of your Bitcoins. You should NOT store all your Bitcoins in your spending wallet and you should have several different spending wallets so that you can make different purchases from different wallets and they won't be linked together.

As you can see, Bitcoin anonymity has its price in time, money, and effort. Relative anonymity is possible, but certainly not easy. Now that you know how, here is a list of places to spend your Bitcoins: *https://en.bitcoin.it/wiki/Trade*. You can now anonymously purchase virtual 3d art (*http://mattgoerzen.tumblr.com/*), VPN service (*https://en.bitcoin.it/wiki/Trade#VPN_Services*), or hosting service (*https://en.bitcoin.it/wiki/Trade#Web_Hosting*).

Rob Robideau

Anonymous Publishing

You should be wary of promoting or recommending your own anonymous posts or publications with an identity that can be linked to you, especially if you are the first or only person recommending a particular publication. This can link your anonymous publication to your real identity.

You can post anonymously on message boards and forums, but a new and truly anonymous account has very little sway in such environments. You can also use clean and unlinked email addresses to send links to your publications to journalists, editors, or blogs that may be interested in sharing your work.

Remember that the content of your publication can often give away your identity just as easily as an unmasked IP address or an email address that was used for something connected to your real identity. Many writers unwittingly reference the local geography, information about a spouse or child, local weather patterns, local flora and fauna, etc. This information can be used to narrow down a search for your real identity.

Most people are aware of the different words that are used by people in the UK versus the US. Words like cookie or biscuit, trunk or boot, or specialize and specialise can bewray your country of residence or origin. Even within a particular country, your reference to particular words, phrases, foods, traditions, cultural nuances, styles, brands, restaurants, etc. can provide clues as to your location, race, religion, upbringing, etc.

More astute observers can take note of your writing patterns and compare them to articles or books that you may have written in the past in connection to your real identity. What phrases do you use most often? Do you have preferred adjectives or adverbs that you use often? What is your preferred sentence structure for certain types of thoughts?

While these observations require a unique combination of time, attention to detail, and research, it is important to note that these are clues that practically anyone can pick up on. It doesn't even require a warrant or an expensive private investigator.

Before publishing, you should scour your work and attempt to remove any words or references that could reveal personal information. You can also go through your work with a thesaurus and replace various words with random synonyms to obscure your writing style. Changing your sentence structures can be more difficult, but try changing random sentences around in a way that doesn't change the meaning. You can change sentences with active voice to passive voice and vice versa.

Even if your writing style is completely obscured, you need to make sure that you are not publishing information that people know only you possess. If you are a whistle-blower at your job, you need to make sure that you don't release information that only you possess or that can be traced back to you. If you are one of only a few experts in a particular field, make sure that you dumb down your information so that it doesn't seem to be coming from that small group of experts.

If you must publish information that can be traced back to you, you might want to stage a plausible information breach some time before the actual publication of the information. It could be as innocuous as several well-documented conversations with co-workers or colleagues or as nefarious as a staged break-in or lost phone or hard drive. This will provide a somewhat plausible imaginary scapegoat if the information itself leads investigators back to you.

The key to remaining anonymous while publishing lies in setting up the publishing accounts using only email accounts, information, and IP addresses that cannot be connected to you as well ensuring sure that the content of the publication itself doesn't lead back to you alone.

Blogs

There are a number of free publishing platforms that you can use to publish on the web. Wordpress (*http://wordpress.com/*), Blogger (*http://www.blogger.com/*), and Tumblr (*https://www.tumblr.com/*) are a few of the most well-known names.

Free publishing platforms have the advantage of not being linked to your bank account or a credit card, but they still require information like your email address and age. I was able to use the preconfigured Tor browser to set up accounts with these services. For maximum anonymity, you should still set up the account from an off-site internet connection that is not linked to you.

Once the account is setup and configured, all of these services will allow you to post to your blog via email. Be sure to use a clean and unlinked email address that is only used for publishing to the blog and never accessed using your real IP address.

Here are instructions for publishing to each of these platforms via email:

- Publishing to Wordpress.com via email
  http://codex.wordpress.org/Post_to_your_blog_using_em ail

- Publishing to Blogger via email
  https://support.google.com/blogger/answer/41452?hl=en

- Publishing to Tumblr via email
  http://www.tumblr.com/docs/en/email_publishing

If you are worried about these free services shutting your blog down over controversial material, you might consider setting up a blog with several different free services and post to all of them each time you want to publish something.

If you don't feel like entrusting the publication of your material to a free service, you can use a self-hosted account to publish. Most of these are paid services, so you will need to use the methods outlined in the section on anonymous financial transactions. While possible, anonymously setting up your own hosting account is tedious and in the end, there is no guarantee that your hosting provider wouldn't suspend your service based on public or government pressure.

On Amazon

You can publish pseudonymously on Amazon, but because Amazon is bent on the whole "making money" thing, there is a lot of verifiable information that is required and I don't believe it is possible to legally publish in a truly anonymous manner.

Amazon's publishing program: *http://kdp.amazon.com/*

Before publishing an ebook on amazon, they require tax information (*https://kdp.amazon.com/self-publishing/help?topic Id=201274750*) so that they can let Uncle Sam know about all the money you will be raking in. They want a taxpayer ID number and the address that the IRS has associated with it.

If you really don't care about the money and don't mind skirting the law, you could use false, yet properly formatted information and just have them send any royalty checks to a bogus address. If you originally set up the account properly and properly hide your real IP address and use a clean email address , there would theoretically be no link back to you.

On the more legal side of things, you can properly set up the account with your real banking and tax information, but publish under a pen name. On the product page and in the Amazon search engine, the book will never be linked to your real name. Yes, Amazon knows behind the scenes who actually published the book and who they need to give the royalties to, but the general public is none the wiser.

One long-shot option that you could consider, is finding

someone to publish on your behalf. If you can get in touch with an Amazon.com published author in an anonymous manner and convince them to publish your book for you, you can get the information out there anonymously. Again, don't expect to make money off of it and the publisher could take it down later for any reason, but at least your story or book would be available on one of the world's largest search engines.

For those who are truly concerned about anonymity, legality, and making money, publishing via Amazon is not really a viable option.

Paper Books or Newsletters

Printing your political documents at home on your desktop printer may seem quite simple and anonymous, but most printers have idiosyncrasies that make them unique and identifiable (*http://33bits.org/2011/10/11/everything-has-a-fingerprint-%E2% 80%94-dont-forget-scanners-and-printers/*). Even if your printer was physically able to output documents that were identical to those coming out of any other printer, there is still the issue of printers purposefully inserting information about your specific printer serial number onto each printed page via a pattern of barely discernable yellow dots. This video from the EFF explains the hidden dots in more detail: *http://youtu.be/izMGMsIZK4U.*

A simple method to print several books or newsletters would be to hire a stranger off the street to take your USB stick with your book files down to the local print shop for printing and pay with cash.

Even if you find a way to anonymously print, another real challenge lies in the distribution of a physical product like a book or newsletter. Publishing has two parts: the preparation and the distribution

pub·lish
/ˈpəbliSH/ ◀)

verb

1. (of an author or company) prepare and issue (a book, journal, piece of music, or other work) for public sale.
   "we publish practical reference books"
   synonyms: issue, bring out, produce, print   More

2. LAW
   communicate (a libel) to a third party.

That pile of books or pamphlets stacked in your basement won't do you any good if you can't get them into the hands of interested parties. Usually this requires some actual legwork on your part. It's time to hit the streets at night in a dark hoodie and tape or staple up your newsletter in places where interested parties will be able to find it. Leave small stacks at convenience stores or wherever people will take them.

Be sure that your physical distribution method does not create a discernable pattern on a map that will point people to your residence. Because books are more expensive, you probably don't want to spread them about randomly. You could leave them on the doorsteps of people that you think would be interested. You could also pay cash and hire someone off the street to mail them to specific people that you think might be interested.

YouTube

YouTube accounts are attached to Google accounts. Google accounts are some of the most difficult to obtain anonymously because of all the verifications that are required. If you follow the suggestions in the earlier section on verifications, you should be able to set up an anonymous Google account that will give you a YouTube account.

Before uploading videos, make sure that you have scrubbed the EXIF data that can give information about the exact date and time that the video was taken, GPS data(if taken with a GPS enabled mobile phone), camera make and model, etc.

The more information that people can collect about the tools you used to record or edit a video, the smaller the pool of suspects gets. EXIF data alone can narrow it down to people at a specific place at a specific time using a specific type of recording device. Depending on the exact file type, you should be able to use EXIFTool (*http://www.sno.phy.queensu.ca/~phil/exiftool/*) to edit the metadata. Beware! This app has no graphical user interface and requires some study to use it effectively, but it is so powerful that you owe it to yourself to take the time to learn it.

Just like in any other type of content, you should make sure that there are no hints or clues that would give away your location or other personal data. We have all see the police procedural shows where people hear the church bells in the background of the audio or recognize a unique type of tree that only grows in a small area and use these clues to locate the uploader.

If you feel compelled to include a voice, make sure that it is not your own. You can alter your voice using free mobile apps or programs like Audacity (*http://audacity.sourceforge.net/*), but the best option would be to use a program that synthesizes a voice from scratch. No, it will not be the most pleasant sounding voice or have perfect inflection, but it will not be linked back to you. A free program called eSpeak (*http://espeak.sourceforge.net/*) is easy to work with and provides a surprisingly clear and understandable voice.

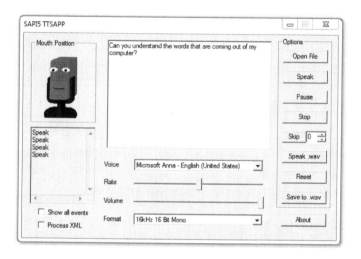

You can even take this a step further with software like CrazyTalk (*http://www.reallusion.com/crazytalk/crazytalk.aspx*) from Reallusion($30). The software can turn any photo into an animation that looks surprisingly lifelike. It can automatically match the animation to an audio track you provide or create its own from your text.

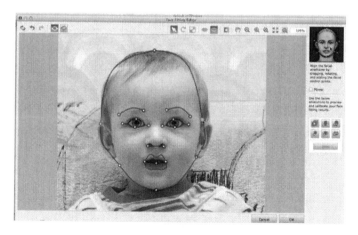

This will allow you to create an anonymous video that is much more likely to grab people's attention and get your point across.

On the other hand, you might want to avoid fancy edits with lots of special effects. If you do too much of that, investigators may be able to determine what editing software you are using and narrow down their pool of suspects based on purchasers or known users of a particular piece of software. To limit liability, make sure you reference the section on anonymous financial transactions before purchasing software.

If you are sharing footage of an event or incident that you have recorded, be aware that investigators may be able to determine where you were located while shooting the footage and look for surveillance cameras that may have caught you while recording.

If you aren't careful, the content alone of your video will breach your anonymity.

Using Social Networks

I know, I know! It's sacrilege to speak of using social network sites in a book about privacy, anonymity, and security. Please do not take this section as an endorsement or encouragement to use social networks, however, the reality of the situation is that many people are addicted to their social networks. Human beings often crave interaction with other human beings and more and more, that interaction is happening online.

While using social networks is in no way advantageous to your privacy, anonymity, or security, if you are set on using them, there are a few steps you can take to limit your exposure.

Feel free to lie to the site or withhold whatever information you wish. I realize that this sounds super obvious, but many people look at their Facebook profile as if it was a banking form that had to be filled out in its entirety. Feel free to use a nickname or even an online handle that many people know you by instead of your real, legal name. Feel free to simply ignore data fields asking for your birthday, phone number, or other information that you don't feel like providing.

Privacy Settings

When you first setup the account, check your privacy settings. These settings are often hidden away and confusing, but you should make sure that your information is not publicly viewable. Remember that almost always, your profile photo is public. This photo is often sucked into and used by other services if you sign into them using the social network. This means that your profile photo will often end up being publicly available on the internet. If you are comfortable with that, pick a photo that makes you look good and put your best foot forward. If not, feel free to use an image that is completely unlinked to you like a simple pattern, a nature photo, or a random photo.

You need to understand that when you tag a friend in a photo, that photo will most likely be visible to all his friends. You should make sure that only you can tag your own photos, otherwise a friend could accidentally tag himself in a private photo of yours and make it visible to all his friends and possibly public if he sets it as his profile photo.

You might want to make sure that your settings don't allow friends to write on your Facebook wall. I'm sure your friends may mean well, but they may come and post Happy Birthday messages on your wall when you may not want to reveal your real date of birth to all your friends. Other information can innocuously and accidentally be revealed by well-meaning, yet uninformed friends.

Once you have your privacy settings setup how you want, you should visit your social network profile with your browser in incognito mode. This simulates someone from the general public visiting your profile without being logged in and should show you what information, if any, is publicly visible.

Sharing Photos

One of the most common activities on social networking sites is sharing photos. I'm sure the grandparents are clamoring to see those cute photos of the little ones, but what if that fantastic, adorable photo you snapped happens to be of your child waving around your credit card after stealing your wallet? You could obviously, just delete the photo, but there are several things you can do to protect your personal information before sharing the photo.

Unintended Sharing

Sometimes, you may not necessarily be aware that you are even sharing at all when it comes to photos. Not all phone menus or social network site warnings include the details of the privacy implications of the action that you are about to take. You may end up accidentally sharing a personal photo without even knowing it if you don't take the time to learn the software and sharing mechanisms in advance.

On a site like Pinterest, you may not even think of the fact that your pinned photos are almost always publicly viewable. Their front page says "Save all the stuff you love", not "share". It's an easy assumption to make.

Most of the time, this isn't a big deal on Pinterest because people aren't often pinning photos that they have taken, but my wife has accurately predicted several unannounced pregnancies based on public Pinterest boards with an inordinate amount of new pregnancy related pins.

You can set up private boards in Pinterest to collect photos of a personal nature that you don't want people to use to draw conclusions. It's probably a good idea to use this feature for most of your boards by default.

Blurring or cropping personal information

Simple, free, and lightweight programs like Irfanview (*http://www.irfanview.com/*) allow you to blur certain portions of the photo or just crop them out. You could even do this to faces if you don't want them to appear in your social media account.

First, click and hold the left(main) mouse button and drag it to draw a rectangle over the area that you want to blur out. When you have drawn the box over the area you want to blur, press, CTRL+E. This will open the image effects browser. From the list on the left, you should select "Pixelize" and use the slider to make sure that that portion of the photo is appropriately distorted.

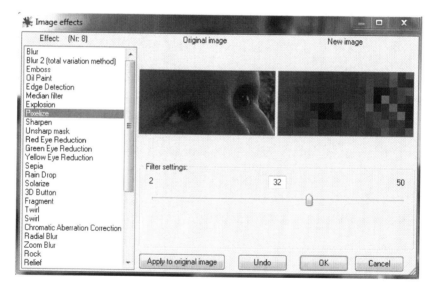

In this example, I used pixelation on my son's eyes:

If you want to crop the image (make it smaller by trimming the edges), simply click and drag the mouse over the image to select the area that you want to keep. When you have selected the correct area, press CTRL+Y.

When you edit the photo, don't forget to save your changes.

Scrubbing EXIF Metadata

Your photos contain more information than just the pixels you see in most photo viewers or editors. The following data was automatically associated with this image taken with a mobile phone:

Camera Make SAMSUNG	**GPS Altitude** 1254
Camera Model GT-I9300	**Unique ID** 761474ab8a47e6d3671f657436ef2be6
Camera Date 2012:11:15 13:11:15	**Online Photo ID** 512dbe3cb804e0d2
Digitized Date 2012:11:15 13:11:15	**X Resolution** 72
Modified Date 2013:02:19 15:01:16+05:45	**Y Resolution** 72
File Date 11/15/2012 1:11:15 PM	**Resolution Unit** Inches
Flash Not Used	**Software** I9300XXBLH1
Focal Length 3.7mm	**Artist** Picasa
Exposure Time 0.000368732s (1/2712)	**YCbCr Positioning** Centered
Aperture 2.76	**Components Configuration** (4 bytes)
F Number f/2.6	**Shutter Speed** 11.4
ISO 80	**Brightness** 9.64
White Balance Auto	**Exposure Bias** 0
Metering Mode Average	**Max Aperture** 2.76
Exposure Program Aperture Priority	**Flashpix Version** (4 bytes)
Color Space sRGB	**Exposure Mode** Auto
Thumbnail (160 x 180 pixels)	**Scene Capture Type** Standard
	GPS Version ID 2.2.0.0
	GPS Altitude Ref 0
	GPS Time Stamp 7, 26, 11
	GPS Processing Method (8 bytes)
JPEG Quality 96 (422)	**GPS Date Stamp** 2012:11:15
GPS Latitude 27 38\'34" N	**Interoperability Index** R98
GPS Longitude 85 17\'26" E	**Related Image Dimensions** 2048 x 1536 pixels

132

This is called the EXIF data. You can see all kinds of information from exact GPS coordinates and camera settings to the exact time the photo was taken and the make and model of the phone used to take the photo. In the wrong hands, this data could be used to stalk you or attack your specific mobile device. In some cases, even when the main photo is edited, the small thumbnail in the EXIF data remains unchanged and reveals the portions of the photo that the editor attempted to remove or pixelate.

If you are sharing a photo, you should strip away the EXIF data so that you aren't giving away more information than necessary. There are several tools you can use to do this. If you are using an Android mobile device, you should look at PhotoInfoEraser (*https://play.google.com/store/apps/details?id=com.yamagoya.and roid.photoinfoeraser.activity&hl=en*). This free app will create a new copy of the image with no EXIF data. The iTunes app Exif Remover (*https://itunes.apple.com/us/app/exif-remover/id477212849?mt=8*) simply strips away the EXIF data and costs $.99. Exif Data Viewer (*http://www.exifdataviewer.com/*) is a free Windows program that allows you to see your EXIF data and edit certain fields.

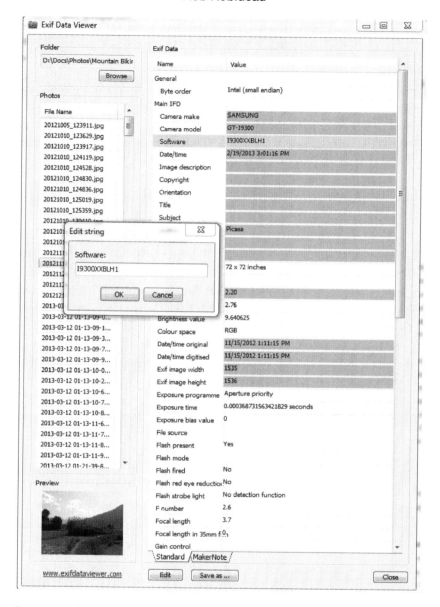

Only the blue highlighted fields are able to be edited. This program does not allow me to edit the GPS information.

On a windows computer, you can use JPG & PNG Stripper (*http://www.steelbytes.com/?mid=30*) to strip the EXIF data from a large number of images all at once. All you have to do is drag in the files that you want to strip and it is done automatically.

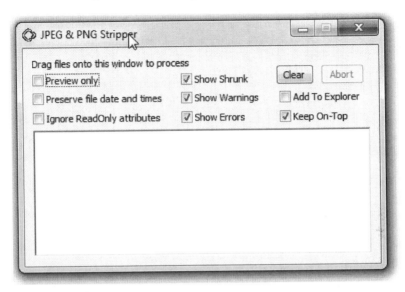

This program consistently stripped most of the data, but unfortunately, I found that even after stripping all the other data, the GPS data remained. EXIF data viewer didn't show the GPS location data, but Picasa (*http://picasa.google.com/*) did. Picasa is the only program I have found that is able to both alter and erase the EXIF GPS location data.

To work with a photo's GPS location data, first select the photo, then click on the little waypoint icon in the lower right corner of the application.

This opens up a map sidebar showing the location that is currently attached to the photo.

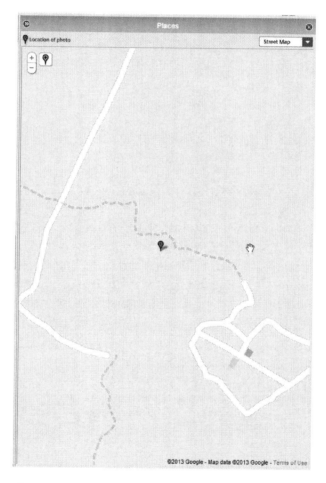

At this point, you can click on the waypoint on the map and it will open a small dialogue box that will offer you the option to "Erase location info". If you click on the link, it does just that.

If you want to edit the location information, you can click and drag the waypoint to a new location on the map and let go. The new GPS data will show that location.

These tools should allow you to make sure that you aren't accidentally leaking personal data through the EXIF data of photos you share via email or social networks.

Social Network "Friends"

If you want to maintain some semblance of privacy and security when it comes to social networking, you should devise your own "friending" policy before starting. Many people seem to get into a race or contest to collect as many "friends" as possible. This is irresponsible behavior when it comes to privacy.

You will need to create your own policy to determine who you want to share your personal information with, but be aware that there are people that want your personal information and are adept at using social networks to get it. I read an article this last year about research companies that are hired to research potential NFL draft picks. These are young men in a very pivotal stage of life and the teams wanted as much information as possible to make an educated decision before betting millions of dollars and the future of their franchises on them.

These research companies created false social networking profiles with the express purpose of deceiving these young men into accepting them as "friends". In some cases, they impersonated real people that the targets knew and were already friends with. The targets didn't first check with the friend that they were already friends with, but rather just accepted the friend request. In other cases, they merely created a new false profile and first targeted friends of the target. When they then sent a friend request to the actual target, they had numerous "mutual friends" and the target often accepted based only on that.

Who is to say that scammers, prospective business partners, or potential employers aren't using these same methods to spy on you? Do you really want them to know about and possibly discriminate against you because of your personal life, family, or religious and political views? Often, employers aren't allowed to ask certain questions on a job application because they aren't allowed to use that information to decide whether or not to hire you, but if they find out the information in another manner, they can use that to inform their decision and blame the choice on some other reason.

To make sure that we don't fall into the same trap, always do some sort of vetting before accepting friend requests. Even sending a simple message to the person asking innocuous questions that would verify their real identity can go a long way toward making sure that you don't end up with fake "friends" with ulterior motives. If the request is coming from a real person that really wants to stay in touch with you, they won't mind verifying their identity or chatting with you!

Be careful and look at every friend request with suspicion. Remember, this isn't a friend-collecting contest!

Conclusion

You made it to the end! Thank you for purchasing this book and taking the time to read it! I sincerely hope that the resources and commentary that you found here were a help. If you enjoyed the book please let others know by reviewing the book:

IncognitoToolkitReviews.com

If you have any questions, suggestions, concerns, or flowery, congratulatory praise, I can be personally reached by emailing *robrobideau@gmail.com*

Other books that I have written include:

***Tactical Bible Stories* - Personal Security Tips from the Bible**
http://www.amazon.com/gp/product/B0082046UK/ref=as_li_ss_t
l?ie=UTF8&camp=1789&creative=390957&creativeASIN=B0082
046UK&linkCode=as2&tag=persoarmampod-20

***Ultralight Survival* - Make a Small and Light Bug Out Bag That Could Save Your Life**
http://www.amazon.com/gp/product/B0093N7T4K/ref=as_li_ss_t
l?ie=UTF8&camp=1789&creative=390957&creativeASIN=B0093
N7T4K&linkCode=as2&tag=persoarmampod-20

***At Home Anywhere* - Six Proven Expat Secrets For Making Yourself At Home in Any Foreign Country**
http://www.amazon.com/gp/product/B007JVRWJU/ref=as_li_ss
_tl?ie=UTF8&camp=1789&creative=390957&creativeASIN=B007
JVRWJU&linkCode=as2&tag=persoarmampod-20

Bideshi Biker - A Short Story About Mountain Biking In Nepal
http://www.amazon.com/gp/product/B00BACRHEY/ref=as_li_ss
_tl?ie=UTF8&camp=1789&creative=390957&creativeASIN=B00B
ACRHEY&linkCode=as2&tag=persoarmampod-20

Practical Guide To Everyday Carry Gear
http://www.amazon.com/gp/product/B006WUQD62/ref=as_li_ss
_tl?ie=UTF8&camp=1789&creative=390957&creativeASIN=B006
WUQD62&linkCode=as2&tag=persoarmampod-20

Appendices

Recommended Browser Extensions

For Google Chrome

Scriptsafe

*https://chrome.google.com/webstore/detail/scriptsafe/oiigbmna
adbkfbmpbfijlflahbdbdgdf?hl=en*

Allows you to block Javascript by default and create a whitelist of trusted domains.

AdblockPlus

https://chrome.google.com/webstore/detail/adblock-
plus/cfhdojbkjhnklbpkdaibdccddilifddb?hl=en

Enjoy surfing the web without obtrusive ads cluttering your
screen.

Ghostery

https://chrome.google.com/webstore/detail/ghostery/mlomiejdfk olichcflejclcbmpeaniij?hl=en

See who's tracking your web browsing with Ghostery.

Mailvelope

*https://chrome.google.com/webstore/detail/mailvelope/kajibbejl
bohfaggdiogboambcijhkke?hl=en*

Secure email with OpenPGP encryption for Webmail.

SwitchySharp

https://chrome.google.com/webstore/detail/proxy-switchysharp/dpplabbmogkhghncfbfdeeokoefdjegm?hl=en

Manage and switch between multiple proxies quickly & easily.
Great for using TOR.

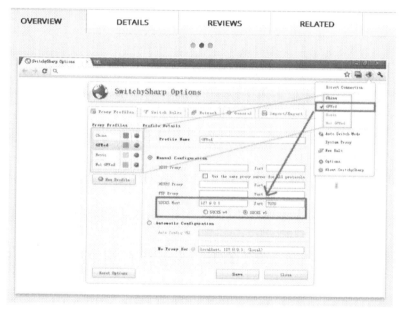

Lastpass

https://chrome.google.com/webstore/detail/lastpass/hdokiejnpi makedhajhdlcegeplioahd?hl=en

LastPass is a free password manager and form filler.

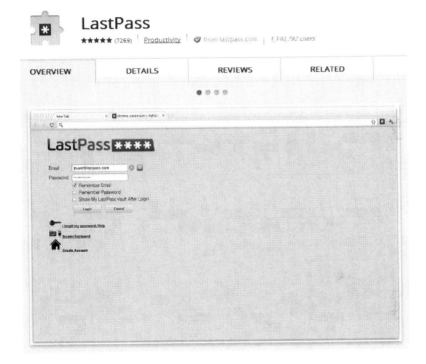

KB SSL Enforcer

https://chrome.google.com/webstore/detail/kb-ssl-enforcer/flcpelgcagfhfoegekianiofphddckof?hl=en

Automatically detects if a site supports SSL (TLS) and enforces all subsequent requests to be over SSL.

WOT (Web of Trust)

https://chrome.google.com/webstore/detail/wot/bhmmomiinigof kjcapegjjndpbikblnp?hl=en

WOT helps you find trustworthy websites based on millions of users' experiences.

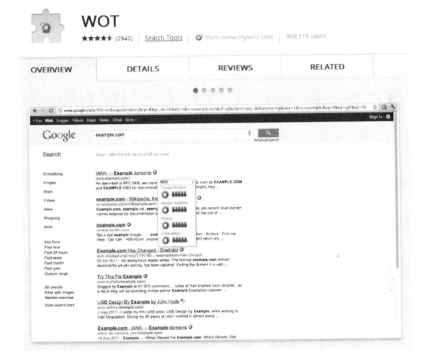

Vanilla Cookie Manager

https://chrome.google.com/webstore/detail/vanilla-cookie-manager/gieohaicffldbmiilohhggbidhephnjj?hl=en

A Cookie Whitelist Manager that helps protect your privacy. Automatically removes unwanted cookies.

Safer Chrome

https://chrome.google.com/webstore/detail/saferchrome/lgpkjjin
gioekjianemgdobchenebhek

SaferChrome makes browsing safer by identifying and
preventing security and privacy breaches.

DoNotTrackMe

https://chrome.google.com/webstore/detail/donottrackme/epanfj
kfahimkgomnigadpkobaefekcd?hl=en

DoNotTrackMe protects your privacy by blocking online
tracking.

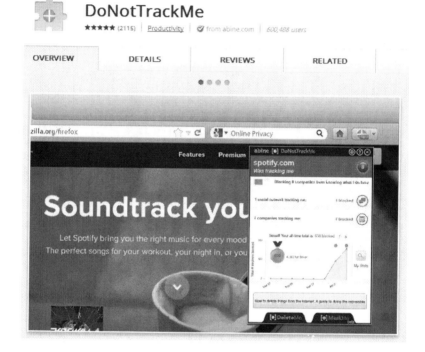

MaskMe

https://chrome.google.com/webstore/detail/maskme/dpkiidbpeij
naaacjlfnijncdlkicejg?hl=en

MaskMe creates disposable email addresses, phone numbers, and credit cards, so now you can enjoy all the web has to offer without giving away your personal data in exchange.

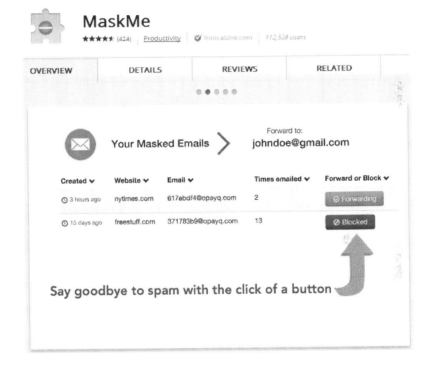

Collusion

https://chrome.google.com/webstore/detail/collusion-for-chrome/ganlifbpkcplnldliibcbegplfmcfigp?hl=en

Visualize and, optionally, block the invisible websites that track you.

BugMeNot

https://chrome.google.com/webstore/detail/bugmenot-lite/lackfehpdclhclidcbbfcemcpolgdgnb?hl=en

Use a community-collected database of login information to access pages without having to provide your own information.

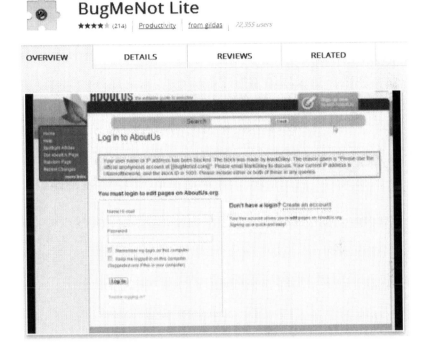

Rob Robideau

HTTPS Everywhere
https://www.eff.org/https-everywhere

For Mozilla Firefox

DoNotTrackMe
https://addons.mozilla.org/en-US/firefox/addon/donottrackplus/

NoScript
https://addons.mozilla.org/en-US/firefox/addon/noscript/

FoxyProxy
https://addons.mozilla.org/en-US/firefox/addon/foxyproxy-standard/

Lastpass

https://addons.mozilla.org/en-US/firefox/addon/lastpass-password-manager/

LastPass Password Manager 2.0.20
by LastPass

LastPass is a free online password manager and Form Filler that makes your web browsing easier and more secure. Also for IE, Safari and Chrome. Your sensitive data is encrypted _locally_ before upload so even LastPass cannot get access to it.
Privacy Policy

HTTPS Everywhere

https://www.eff.org/https-everywhere

Collusion

https://addons.mozilla.org/en-US/firefox/addon/collusion/

Collusion 0.27 NO RESTART
by Jono X, Dethe Elza

Visualize who's tracking you in real time. To get started, click on the Collusion icon in the bottom-right corner of your browser. (You may need to show the Add-on Bar to see the icon.)

Download Now

BugMeNot

https://addons.mozilla.org/en-US/firefox/addon/bugmenot/

Rob Robideau

Recommended Applications

Portable Software (USB)

Full List of Available Portable Apps
http://portableapps.com/apps

Keepass - Password Safe
http://portableapps.com/apps/utilities/keepass_portable

7-Zip - File Archiver
http://portableapps.com/apps/utilities/7-zip_portable

Notepad++ - Simple, Lightweight Text Editor
http://portableapps.com/apps/development/notepadpp_portable

VLC - Simple, Lightweight Media Player
http://portableapps.com/apps/music_video/vlc_portable

Irfanview - Image Viewer
*http://portableapps.com/apps/graphics_pictures/irfanview_porta
ble*

GIMP - Image Editor
http://portableapps.com/apps/graphics_pictures/gimp_portable

Sumatra - PDF Viewer
http://portableapps.com/apps/office/sumatra_pdf_portable

Foxit - PDF Viewer
http://portableapps.com/apps/office/foxit_reader_portable

Eraser - Secure File and Data Deletion
http://portableapps.com/apps/utilities/eraser_portable

Portable StenoG - Hide Files in Images
http://www.softpedia.com/get/PORTABLE-
SOFTWARE/Security/Encrypting/Windows-Portable-
Applications-Portable-SteganoG.shtml

Mobile Apps

Android

Applock

https://play.google.com/store/apps/details?id=com.domobile.ap plock

Applock allows you to secure specific apps with a password. You can also lock incoming calls so that strangers can't answer your phone, lock the Play Store, Settings, and prevent installs and uninstalls. There are additional premium features that require a subscription($.99/mo or $2.99/yr), but the app is quite functional without the subscription.

Autowipe

https://play.google.com/store/apps/details?id=com.vesperaNovu s.app.AutowipeFree

This app allows you to automatically wipe the device in several different situations. If an incorrect password is entered for the phone x amount of times, it can autowipe. You can set the amount of times. If the subscriber ID is changed (SIM card is changed), it can automatically wipe the device. If a text with a specific passphrase is received, it can autowipe the device. You can also set it to clear the SD if you wish. The app itself can be password protected so that strangers cannot disable your settings.

APG

https://play.google.com/store/apps/details?id=org.thialfihar.andr oid.apg

This app allows you to encrypt and decrypt messages and files via PGP. It can store public and private keys and has a pretty simple interface.

ProXPN VPN

*https://play.google.com/store/apps/details?id=com.proxpn.prox
pn*

OpenVPN app for the service, ProXPN.

Orbot: Proxy With TOR

https://play.google.com/store/apps/details?id=org.torproject.android

This app allows you to browse the internet with greater anonymity. It functions much like the desktop TOR client.

BitTorrent Sync

https://play.google.com/store/apps/details?id=com.bittorrent.sync

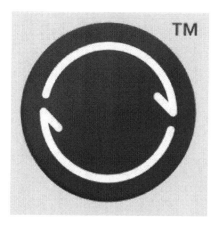

The Android mobile client for BitTorrent Sync that allows you to synchronize data across devices without relying on a cloud service provider like Dropbox

---

Cloudfogger
https://play.google.com/store/apps/details?id=com.cloudfogger.
cf

This app is a mobile interface for accessing encrypted files that you have stored on Dropbox via your Cloudfogger desktop app.

Viivo

https://play.google.com/store/apps/details?id=com.pkware.viivo

This app is a mobile interface for accessing encrypted files that you have stored on Dropbox via your Viivo desktop app.

BoxCryptor

*https://play.google.com/store/apps/details?id=com.boxcryptor.a
ndroid*

This app is a mobile interface for accessing encrypted files that you have stored on Dropbox via your BoxCryptor desktop app.

Lookout Security and Antivirus
https://play.google.com/store/apps/details?id=com.lookout

This app scans and protects from viruses, malware, adware, and spyware. It also offers helpful features to locate your phone by making it scream or turning on the GPS from a web interface for locating it remotely. It can also take a photo with the front facing camera if an incorrect password is entered 3 times and email it to you along with the phone's location. It also offers premium services with a subscription, but all the above mentioned features are free.

Lastpass

https://play.google.com/store/apps/details?id=com.lastpass.lpan droid

This app allows you to access your Lastpass vault with all your passwords. It also has a browser that can automatically enter your passwords on most websites.

Wifi Finder

https://play.google.com/store/apps/details?id=com.jiwire.androi d.finder

Scan for wifi hotspots or used their mapped database of over 850,000 hotspots.

Titanium Backup

*https://play.google.com/store/apps/details?id=com.keramidas.Ti
taniumBackup*

If you have your phone set up to remote wipe in various situations, you need to make sure that your phone is properly backed up. Titanium backup allows you to make very secure backups of your phone and even encrypt the files with a passphrase that only you keep track of before storing them on various cloud storage services. If you use the encryption settings, all encryption and decryption is done on your device and all files are encrypted before transit and storage in the cloud.

Redphone
*https://play.google.com/store/apps/details?id=org.thoughtcrime.
redphone*

This app offers encrypted voice calls from a mobile device over wifi or your cell data network. Don't count on this to keep you secure from a sophisticated digital hacker, but at least your conversations are not broadcast in the clear for anyone to intercept with simple radio devices.

Gibberbot

https://play.google.com/store/apps/details?id=info.guardianproje ct.otr.app.im

This app uses Off-The-Record (OTR) encryption to secure your messages in transit. It can communicate with other OTR compatible messaging apps like ChatSecure, Adium, or Pidgin.

IOS

BitTorrent Sync
https://itunes.apple.com/us/app/bittorrent-sync/id665156116?ls=1&mt=8

The Android mobile client for BitTorrent Sync that allows you to synchronize data across devices without relying on a cloud service provider like Dropbox

---

ProXPN VPN

https://itunes.apple.com/us/app/proxpn-vpn/id546557458?mt=8

OpenVPN app for the service, ProXPN.

Lastpass

https://itunes.apple.com/us/app/lastpass-for-premium-customers/id324613447?mt=8

This app allows you to access your Lastpass vault with all your passwords. It also has a browser that can automatically enter your passwords on most websites.

Lookout Mobile Security

https://itunes.apple.com/us/app/lookout-backup-security-find/id434893913?mt=8

This app scans and protects from viruses, malware, adware, and spyware. It also offers helpful features to locate your phone by making it scream or turning on the GPS from a web interface for locating it remotely. It can also take a photo with the front facing camera if an incorrect password is entered 3 times and email it to you along with the phone's location. It also offers premium services with a subscription, but all the above mentioned features are free.

Viivo

https://itunes.apple.com/us/app/viivo/id557540030?mt=8

This app is a mobile interface for accessing encrypted files that you have stored on Dropbox via your Viivo desktop app.

WiFi Finder

https://itunes.apple.com/en/app/wi-fi-finder/id300708497?mt=8

Scan for wifi hotspots or used their mapped database of over 850,000 hotspots.

Cloudfogger

https://itunes.apple.com/us/app/cloudfogger-cloud-encryption/id522342963?mt=8

This app is a mobile interface for accessing encrypted files that you have stored on Dropbox via your Cloudfogger desktop app.

BoxCryptor
https://itunes.apple.com/us/app/boxcryptor-classic/id484546808?mt=8

This app is a mobile interface for accessing encrypted files that you have stored on Dropbox via your BoxCryptor desktop app.

ChatSecure
https://itunes.apple.com/us/app/chatsecure-encrypted-secure/id464200063?mt=8

Encrypted, Secure Multi-protocol Chat and Instant Messaging (Google Talk, XMPP, OSCAR)

Onion Browser

https://itunes.apple.com/us/app/onion-browser/id519296448?mt=8

Onion Browser is a Tor-capable web browser that lets you access the internet privately and anonymously.

Rob Robideau

Other Recommended Resources

Security Now Podcast - *http://twit.tv/sn*

http://krebsonsecurity.com/

https://www.schneier.com/

Recommended Books

On Anonymity

Complete Guide to Internet Privacy, Anonymity & Security
http://www.amazon.com/Complete-Internet-Anonymity-Security-ebook/dp/B007L8MZCU/persoarmampod-20

By Matthew Bailey - 2011 - 4.2 out of 5 stars

It's true that technology can be confusing and even intimidating. However, this book contains all the information you need to empower and protect yourself. In this comprehensive and easy-to-read guide for Windows users, you will quickly learn how to:

- surf the Internet freely and get downloads without censorship or restriction,

- prevent identity theft and keep cyber-criminals from hacking into your computer,

- stop search engines, social networking sites and powerful Internet players from tracking and profiling you,

- use encryption to keep your downloads, personal documents and sensitive information 100% hidden and safe,

- use the best (and often free!) privacy, anonymity and security software that really works

- keep your computer free from viruses, worms, trojans, rootkits, email/web bugs, spyware, adware and malware,

- prevent Big Brother, your Internet service provider (ISP) and unwelcome snoops from monitoring you,

- get rid of trace and hidden data on your computer that exposes your private activities, and

- apply all these techniques to areas of special interest such as:

  ➢ whether someone is up to mischief on their computer,

  ➢ safe online shopping,

  ➢ workplace and small office/home office (SOHO) issues, and

  ➢ shielding your children from potential harm.

You will benefit for years to come from your small investment in this book. After all, your privacy and security are priceless.

Both ebook and paperback versions are available

Ebook - $9.99

Hacking the Future: Privacy, Identity, and Anonymity on the Web
http://www.amazon.com/Hacking-the-Future-
ebook/dp/B00A6WPLMY/persoarmampod-20

By Cole Stryker - 2012- 4.0 out of 5 stars

How does anonymity enable free speech - and how is it a threat? "I think anonymity on the Internet has to go away," famously said by Randi Zuckerberg (sister of Mark), has become the policy for some, while the Stop Online Piracy Act mobilized millions to write Congress in protest. Identity Wars is a broad look at how anonymity influences politics, activism, religion, and art.

Stryker presents a strong defense of anonymity and explores some of the tools and organizations relating to this issue, especially as it has evolved with the ubiquity of the Internet. Cogent and compelling, his examination of online identities, both false and real, is an essential read for the social-networking age.

Both ebook and paperback versions are available

Ebook- $12.99

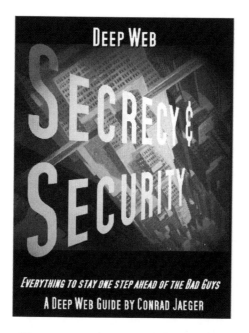

Deep Web Secrecy and Security
http://www.amazon.com/Secrecy-Security-Defeat-Snoopers-ebook/dp/B008KKCXMU/persoarmampod-20

By Conrad Jaeger - 2012 - 4.5 out of 5 stars

This book is chock full of fantastic resources that will have you furiously highlighting, scribbling notes, and following links. While the information is good, the tone does seem a little alarmist or sensational and the "deep web" terminology seemed unnecessary.

The author does a good job explaining subjects that can be quite complicated.

If you are looking to make yourself less vulnerable while using the internet, this book is a wonderful place to start.

Both ebook and paperback versions are available

Ebook - $9.99

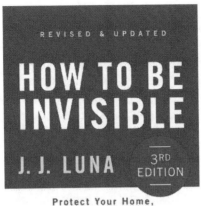

How to Be Invisible: Protect Your Home, Your Children, Your Assets, and Your Life

http://www.amazon.com/How-Be-Invisible-Children-ebook/dp/B0065QZVB6/persoarmampod-20

By J.J. Luna - 2012 - 4.1 out of 5 stars

"Fascinating... a regular field manual... meticulously researched and very entertaining." --G. Gordon Liddy

A thoroughly revised and updated edition of the essential guide to preserving your personal security. From cyberspace to crawl spaces, new innovations in information gathering have left the private life of the average person open to scrutiny, and worse, exploitation. In this thoroughly updated third edition of his immensely popular guide How to Be Invisible, J.J. Luna shows you how to protect your home address, hide your ownership of vehicles and real estate, use pagers with dumbphones, switch to low-profile banking and invisible money transfers, use alternate signatures, and how to secretly run a home-based business.

J.J. Luna is an expert and highly trained security consultant with years of experience protecting himself, his family, and his clients. Using real life stories and his own consulting experience, J.J. Luna divulges legal methods to attain the privacy you crave and deserve, whether you want to shield yourself from casual scrutiny or take your life savings with you and disappear without a trace. Whatever your needs, Luna reveals the shocking secrets that private detectives and other seekers of personal information use to uncover information and then shows how to make a serious commitment to safeguarding yourself.

There is a prevailing sense in our society that true privacy is a thing of the past. In a world where privacy concerns that only continue to grow in magnitude, How to Be Invisible, Third Edition is a critical antidote to the spread of new and more efficient ways of undermining our personal security.

Privacy is a commonly-lamented casualty of the Information Age and of the world's changing climate--but that doesn't mean you have to stand for it. This new edition of J. J. Luna's classic manual contains step-by-step advice on building and maintaining your personal security, including brand new chapters on:

- The dangers from Facebook, smartphones, and facial recognition

- How to locate a nominee (or proxy) you can trust

- The art of pretexting, aka social engineering

- Moving to Baja California Sur; San Miguel de Allende, Guanajuato; Cuenca, Ecuador; or Spain's Canary Islands

- The secrets of international privacy, and much more!

Both ebook and paperback version are available

Ebook - $11.99

How to be Anonymous Online

http://www.amazon.com/dp/B00BDVBGQC/persoarmampod-20

By Anna Eydie - 2013 - 4.3 out of 5 stars

The author's recommendations won't work for every situation, but they do provide a basis for further action and increased awareness concerning the risks and countermeasures when attempting to remain anonymous on the internet. The book contains a well written section that describes how bitcoins are not truly anonymous in a relatively simple manner.

I would prefer that the book provide more options and resources than the limited software recommendations and methods that are covered in this book. Also, a few images/screenshots would be nice during the tutorials.

Overall, I would recommend this book for beginners looking for a quick and easy way to access the internet anonymously.

Only available as an ebook

Ebook - $6.99

How to Purchase Anonymously on the Internet
http://www.amazon.com/How-Purchase-Anonymously-Internet-
ebook/dp/B00538MB2E/persoarmampod-20

By Hank Taggart - 2011 - 5.0 out of 5 stars

The author shares his experiences and what he has found to work. He describes the ins and outs of various types of payments and methods of receiving packages that won't compromise your anonymity. This is not a 1000-foot theoretical overview. The author makes specific recommendations that will work for most people. Highly recommended!

Only available as an Kindle ebook

Ebook - $9.77

Easy Private Browsing

https://www.amazon.com/gp/product/B009IUO1L2/persoarmampod-20

By Max Wilhard - 2013 - 4.5 out of 5 stars

The chapters are broken down into simple "how-tos" like "How to hide your IP address from a web site administrator" or various other tasks. The author offers up detailed tutorials on how to achieve these different tasks in various use cases. The appendix is also fantastic with specific tutorials for clearing cookies and using private browsing modes in different browsers. He also offers up detailed advice for configuring TOR with browsers and email clients.

This book is highly recommended for those that want to learn more about how to control what information they expose while accessing the internet!

Only available as an ebook

Ebook - $9.99

Invisible Money, Secret Assets, Hidden Accounts
http://www.amazon.com/Invisible-Hidden-Assets-Accounts-ebook/dp/B00DF4SH0I/persoarmampod-20

JJ Luna - 2013 - 4.2 out of 5 stars

This book goes into quite a bit of detail on everything from how to handle traffic stops while carrying large amounts of cash to opening bank accounts that will be difficult for investigators to find. The author gives advice that will keep you from raising red flags as you try to manage your money in a manner that will keep it hidden and safe from those that may be after it for nefarious, yet quasi-legal reasons.

This book will offer some insight as to how private investigators work to uncover assets and what you can do to make life difficult for them.

Only available as an ebook

Ebook - $9.99

On Investigation, Background Checks, and Information Gathering

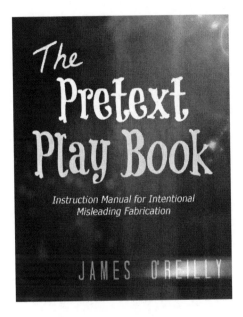

The Pretext Playbook
http://www.amazon.com/Instruction-Intentional-Misleading-Fabrication-ebook/dp/B00BHRMQ3O/persoarmampod-20

By James O'Reilly - 2013 - 4.2 out of 5 stars

Wow! This book showed me how trusting I am and how I could easily be taken advantage of, tracked, or accidentally give out my personal identifiable information without even knowing it. This book can help you protect your privacy in a more effective manner.

This book is highly recommended reading for anyone who wants to understand how the pros go after information and how you keep from falling into the traps.

Only available as an ebook

Ebook - $11.99

Investigator's Little Black Book 3
http://www.amazon.com/Investigators-Little-Black-Book-ebook/dp/B004F9P9YY/persoarmampod-20

By Robert Scott P.I. - 2002 - 4.0 out of 5 stars

This books has an amazing amount of resources for harvesting information. $3 is an amazing deal for the collection of addresses and instructions that are included in this book. Highly recommended for anyone who wants to know more about the variety of information sources that are available to investigators.

Both ebook and paperback versions are available

Ebook - $2.99

Is My Cell Phone Bugged?
https://www.amazon.com/gp/product/B0052Z8FK0/persoarmampod-
20

By Kevin D. Murray - 2011 - 4.3 out of 5 stars

The author goes into detail about what to look for if you suspect that your phone might be bugged and continues to offer up tips for making sure that the equipment you use is not easy to bug. He lays out what exactly is possible when it comes to bugging phones, how it is typically done, how difficult it is, etc.

The author also offers good advice on tangentially related subjects like methods of bugging non-phone conversations.

If you are at all concerned about the security and privacy of your phone communications, you owe it to yourself to read this book and gain some extra knowledge on the subject.
Highly recommended!

Kindle and hardcover versions available

Ebook - $7.69

On Cryptography

The Code Book: The Science of Secrecy from Ancient Egypt to Quantum Cryptography
http://www.amazon.com/Code-Book-Science-Cryptography-ebook/dp/B004IK8PLE/persoarmampod-20

By Simon Singh - 2000 - 4.7 out of 5 stars

In his first book since the bestselling **Fermat's Enigma**, Simon Singh offers the first sweeping history of encryption, tracing its evolution and revealing the dramatic effects codes have had on wars, nations, and individual lives. From Mary, Queen of Scots, trapped by her own code, to the Navajo Code Talkers who helped the Allies win World War II, to the incredible (and incredibly simple) logistical breakthrough that made Internet commerce secure, **The Code Book** tells the story of the most powerful intellectual weapon ever known: secrecy.

Throughout the text are clear technical and mathematical explanations, and portraits of the remarkable personalities who wrote and broke the world's most difficult codes. Accessible, compelling, and remarkably far-reaching, this book will forever alter your view of history and what drives it. It will also make you wonder how private that e-mail you just sent really is.

Both ebook and paperback version are available

Ebook - $13.84

Cracking Codes and Cryptograms for Dummies

http://www.amazon.com/Cracking-Codes-Cryptograms-Dummies-ebook/dp/B005CB22A8/persoarmampod-20

By Denise Sutherland and Mark Koltko-Rivera - 2011 - 4.4 out of 5 stars

As most "For Dummies" books, this book does an excellent job of going very broad to cover a wide variety of subjects related to codes and cryptography. It seems to have everything from history to many examples of early codes and ciphers, but don't expect in-depth commentary on more modern cryptography.

Available in both Kindle and paperback versions

Ebook - $6.99

On Privacy

Why is privacy important? How much privacy is enough?

PRIVACY
IN CONTEXT
Technology, Policy, and the Integrity of Social Life
HELEN NISSENBAUM

Privacy In Context: Technology, Policy, And The Integrity Of Social Life
http://www.amazon.com/Privacy-Context-Stanford-Books-ebook/dp/B005M43916/persoarmampod-20

By Helen Nissenbaum - 2009 - 4.8 Stars

"Privacy is one of the most urgent issues associated with information technology and digital media. This book claims that what people really care about when they complain and protest that privacy has been violated is not the act of sharing information itself—most people understand that this is crucial to social life —but the inappropriate, improper sharing of information.

Arguing that privacy concerns should not be limited solely to concern about control over personal information, Helen Nissenbaum counters that information ought to be distributed and protected according to norms governing distinct social contexts—whether it be workplace, health care, schools, or among family and friends. She warns that basic distinctions between public and private, informing many current privacy policies, in fact obscure more than they clarify. In truth, contemporary information systems should alarm us only when they function without regard for social norms and values, and thereby weaken the fabric of social life."

Both ebook and paperback version are available

Ebook - $18.69

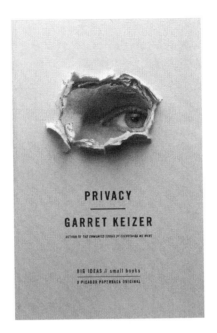

Privacy (Big Ideas//Small Books)
http://www.amazon.com/Privacy-IDEAS-small-books-
ebook/dp/B007TJ5BIG/persoarmampod-20

By Garret Keizer - 2012 - 3.4 out of 5 stars

American essayist and Harper's contributing editor Garret Keizer offers a brilliant, literate look at our strip-searched, over-shared, viral-videoed existence.

Body scans at the airport, candid pics on Facebook, a Twitter account for your stray thoughts, and a surveillance camera on every street corner -- today we have an audience for all of the extraordinary and banal events of our lives. The threshold between privacy and exposure becomes more permeable by the minute. But what happens to our private selves when we cannot escape scrutiny, and to our public personas when they pass from our control?

In this wide-ranging, penetrating addition to the Big Ideas//Small Books series, and in his own unmistakable voice, Garret Keizer considers the moral dimensions of privacy in relation to issues of social justice, economic inequality, and the increasing commoditization of the global marketplace. Though acutely aware of the digital threat to privacy rights, Keizer refuses to see privacy in purely technological terms or as an essentially legalistic value. Instead, he locates privacy in the human capacity for resistance and in the sustainable society "with liberty and justice for all."

Both ebook and paperback version are available

Ebook - $9.99

Understanding Privacy
http://www.amazon.com/Understanding-Privacy-
ebook/dp/B002WTC5BO/persoarmampod-20

By Daniel J. Solove - 2010 - 4.3 out of 5 stars

Privacy is one of the most important concepts of our time, yet it is also one of the most elusive. As rapidly changing technology makes information increasingly available, scholars, activists, and policymakers have struggled to define privacy, with many conceding that the task is virtually impossible.

In this concise and lucid book, Daniel J. Solove offers a comprehensive overview of the difficulties involved in discussions of privacy and ultimately provides a provocative resolution. He argues that no single definition can be workable, but rather that there are multiple forms of privacy, related to one another by family resemblances. His theory bridges cultural differences and addresses historical changes in views on privacy. Drawing on a broad array of interdisciplinary sources, Solove sets forth a framework for understanding privacy that provides clear, practical guidance for engaging with relevant issues.

Understanding Privacy will be an essential introduction to long-standing debates and an invaluable resource for crafting laws and policies about surveillance, data mining, identity theft, state involvement in reproductive and marital decisions, and other pressing contemporary matters concerning privacy.

Both ebook and paperback version are available

Ebook - $15.20

The Players, Regulators, and Stakeholders

Privacy and Big Data

Privacy and Big Data

http://www.amazon.com/Privacy-and-Big-Data-ebook/dp/B005QEBEU0/persoarmampod-20

By Terence Craig - 2011 - 3.7 out of 5 stars

Much of what constitutes Big Data is information about us. Through our online activities, we leave an easy-to-follow trail of digital footprints that reveal who we are, what we buy, where we go, and much more. This eye-opening book explores the raging privacy debate over the use of personal data, with one undeniable conclusion: once data's been collected, we have absolutely no control over who uses it or how it is used.

Personal data is the hottest commodity on the market today—truly more valuable than gold. We are the asset that every company, industry, non-profit, and government wants. Privacy and Big Data introduces you to the players in the personal data game, and explains the stark differences in how the U.S., Europe, and the rest of the world approach the privacy issue.

You'll learn about:

- **Collectors:** social networking titans that collect, share, and sell user data

- **Users:** marketing organizations, government agencies, and many others

- **Data markets:** companies that aggregate and sell datasets to anyone

- **Regulators:** governments with one policy for commercial data use, and another for providing security

Both ebook and paperback version are available

Ebook - $10.59

The Right to Privacy

http://www.amazon.com/Right-Privacy-Vintage-ebook/dp/B0043M4ZBG/persoarmampod-20

By Caroline Kennedy / Ellen Alderman - 1997 -4.6 out of 5 stars

Can the police strip-search a woman who has been arrested for a minor traffic violation? Can a magazine publish an embarrassing photo of you without your permission? Does your boss have the right to read your email? Can a company monitor its employees' off-the-job lifestyles--and fire those who drink, smoke, or live with a partner of the same sex? Although the word privacy does not appear in the Constitution, most of us believe that we have an inalienable right to be left alone. Yet in arenas that range from the battlefield of abortion to the information highway, privacy is under siege. In this eye-opening and sometimes hair-raising book, Alderman and Kennedy survey hundreds of recent cases in which ordinary citizens have come up against the intrusions of government, businesses, the news media, and their own neighbors. At once shocking and instructive, up-to-date and rich in historical perspective, **The Right to Private** is an invaluable guide to one of the most charged issues of our time.

Both ebook and paperback version are available

Ebook -$13.99

Rob Robideau

Rights and Advocacy Organizations

Electronic Frontier Foundation - *www.eff.org*

American Civil Liberties Union - *https://www.aclu.org/*

Electronic Privacy Information Center - *http://epic.org/*

Open Rights Group - *http://www.openrightsgroup.org/*

KEEPING THE INTERNET
OPEN • INNOVATIVE • FREE

CENTER FOR DEMOCRACY
& TECHNOLOGY

Center for Democracy and Technology - *https://www.cdt.org/*

Papers Please - *http://www.papersplease.org/wp/*

Public Knowledge - *http://www.publicknowledge.org/*

Remember

With the right resources, creativity, torture, social engineering, bribery, or betrayal, almost any secret can be revealed. While we recommend that you make every effort to secure your communications and obscure any data collection concerning your online activities, remember that there are no guarantees. While this book contains a wide selection of tools that will help you secure your online activities, the greatest tool is your mind. Think about your goals and use cases and select the tools that will help you accomplish them with the appropriate level of anonymity, security, and convenience. When it comes to privacy, security, and anonymity, there is no single, magical action that will take care of everything. Good security requires you to examine all your habits and your online lifestyle to identify and shore up the vulnerable areas. To remain as secure as possible, you should also keep up with security news so that you will be made aware of new exploits of vulnerabilities that may be discovered in the future. Take responsibility for your own security and stay alert!